Cambridge Elements ≡

Elements in Forensic Linguistics
edited by
Tim Grant
Aston University
Tammy Gales
Hofstra University

DECODING TERRORISM

An Interdisciplinary Approach to a Lone-Actor Case

Julia Kupper
Independent Scholar

Marie Bojsen-Møller
University of Copenhagen

Tanya Karoli Christensen
University of Copenhagen

Dakota Wing
York University

Marcus Papadopulos
Independent Scholar

Sharon Smith
Independent Scholar

CAMBRIDGE
UNIVERSITY PRESS

CAMBRIDGE
UNIVERSITY PRESS

Shaftesbury Road, Cambridge CB2 8EA, United Kingdom

One Liberty Plaza, 20th Floor, New York, NY 10006, USA

477 Williamstown Road, Port Melbourne, VIC 3207, Australia

314–321, 3rd Floor, Plot 3, Splendor Forum, Jasola District Centre, New Delhi – 110025, India

103 Penang Road, #05–06/07, Visioncrest Commercial, Singapore 238467

Cambridge University Press is part of Cambridge University Press & Assessment, a department of the University of Cambridge.

We share the University's mission to contribute to society through the pursuit of education, learning and research at the highest international levels of excellence.

www.cambridge.org
Information on this title: www.cambridge.org/9781009495745

DOI: 10.1017/9781009495738

First published 2024

A catalogue record for this publication is available from the British Library

ISBN 978-1-009-49574-5 Hardback
ISBN 978-1-009-49572-1 Paperback
ISSN 2634-7334 (online)
ISSN 2634-7326 (print)

Decoding Terrorism

An Interdisciplinary Approach to a Lone-Actor Case

Elements in Forensic Linguistics

DOI: 10.1017/9781009495738
First published online: November 2024

Julia Kupper
Independent Scholar

Marie Bojsen-Møller
University of Copenhagen

Tanya Karoli Christensen
University of Copenhagen

Dakota Wing
York University

Marcus Papadopulos
Independent Scholar

Sharon Smith
Independent Scholar

Author for correspondence: Julia Kupper, info@juliakupper.com

Abstract: This Element is an interdisciplinary analysis of the language evidence produced before, during and following a lone-actor terrorism attack that occurred in Halle, Germany, on October 9, 2019, resulting in two casualties. During his final preparations, the perpetrator, twenty-seven-year-old Stephan Balliet, announced his attack online and disseminated a targeted violence manifesto shortly before live-streaming his premeditated act. This post-hoc investigation introduces a multi-method approach that synchronizes well-established qualitative methodologies for forensic text analysis – genre, text linguistics, appraisal and uptake – to elucidate these data types. Furthermore, a retroactive threat assessment based on language data from the trial transcripts provides a holistic review of the assailant's background, red flags, triggering events and warning behaviors that could have signaled his movements along the pathway to violence. The results are considered in an organizational context to highlight current challenges faced by security agencies when mitigating the risk of lone-actors who radicalize in online environments.

Keywords: forensic linguistics, threat assessment, language evidence, far-right terrorism, targeted violence manifesto

ISBNs: 9781009495745 (HB), 9781009495721 (PB), 9781009495738 (OC)
ISSNs: 2634-7334 (online), 2634-7326 (print)

Contents

Series Preface   1

Prologue: Online Radicalization   1

1 Introduction   3

2 Methodology   7

3 Rhetorical Genre Analysis   9

4 Text Linguistic Analysis   19

5 Stance Analysis   29

6 Retrospective Threat Assessment   39

7 Lone-Actor Investigative Challenges   49

8 Contagion and Copycat Uptakes   59

9 Discussion   69

References   74

Series Preface

The Elements in Forensic Linguistics series from Cambridge University Press publishes across four main topic areas: (1) investigative and forensic text analysis; (2) the study of spoken linguistic practices in legal contexts; (3) the linguistic analysis of written legal texts; (4) explorations of the origins, development and scope of the field in various regions. *Decoding Terrorism: An Interdisciplinary Approach to a Lone-Actor Case* by Julia Kupper, Marie Bojsen-Møller, Tanya Karoli Christensen, Dakota Wing, Marcus Papadopulos and Sharon Smith is situated within the first of these categories and offers a retrospective investigation of the linguistic and behavioral evidence produced by the perpetrator prior to and during the catastrophic event in Germany in 2019.

The first Element of its kind in our series, the authors bring a unique constellation of contributions to this case study. First, the authors have lived and worked in a variety of countries, including the US, Canada, Denmark and Germany, among others. With these varied international experiences, they offer a range of cultural perspectives on the evidence in this case. Second, the authors represent a variety of scholarly fields such as linguistics, psychology and criminology. With this scholarly breadth, the authors have drawn on methodologies such as genre analysis, text linguistics, interpersonal stance, behavioral analysis and uptake analysis, providing insights from a range of complementary lenses. Finally, their collective practical experiences include positions in law enforcement and university teaching, involvement in forensic linguistic and behavioral case work and the provision of threat assessment training seminars, all of which contribute to their investigative and academic understanding of threats from serious violent offenders. The results of this impressive case study clearly highlight the benefits of international and interdisciplinary work, and we encourage more collaborative research and practice moving forward.

Tammy Gales
Series Editor

Prologue: Online Radicalization

Since the advent of the internet in the 1980–1990s, cyberspace has become an important venue for radicalization and cross-fertilization of ideological content (Schwarz, 2020; Simi & Windisch, 2020).[1] Violent extremists leverage the global interconnectivity of the virtual sphere to establish and maintain relationships with like-minded individuals and organizations, and facilitate expansions by spreading

---

[1] The main contributor of this section was Julia Kupper.

propaganda to attract and recruit new members (Dittrich et al., 2022; Scrivens et al., 2021). Today's online platforms provide diverse (sub)cultures with extensive opportunities for interaction, enabling the global exchange of content without delay or oversight. Proponents of extreme movements have emerged on all mainstream social media channels to disseminate radical content, including Facebook, Instagram, Twitter (now X), TikTok and YouTube, but also on fringe forums, for instance anonymous imageboard forums such as "the chans" (e.g., 4chan or 8chan). Particularly the far-right[2] – right-wing populists, national conservatives and violent revolutionists – has created a parallel universe of alternative platforms where extreme worldviews appear to be reiterated with discourse that evades content moderation, avoids fact checking and disregards opposing opinions (Fuchs & Middelhoff, 2020). Examples of such platforms include Parler (emulating Facebook), Gab (emulating Twitter – now X), Bitchute (emulating YouTube), Metapedia (emulating Wikipedia) and Voat (emulating Reddit).

The Swedish Defence Research Agency (European Commission, 2021) found that the violent right uses specific jargon to strengthen their members' sense of belonging and to enforce their ideological messaging by utilizing toxic language, dehumanization terminology and conspiracy theories in digital environments. Furthermore, the Institute of Strategic Dialogue (Bedingfield, 2021) observed that major game streaming and messaging platforms, such as Steam, Discord and Twitch, host publicly accessible chat servers, channels and groups that are composed of large networks of radical far-right collectives and extremist activities. In a study across twelve chan sites, the Centre for Research and Evidence on Security Threats (Keen, Crawford & Suarez-Tangil, 2020) found that several imageboards fostered an extremist mindset and promoted violence on the basis of deploying irony and humor in memes and other visual narratives. In addition, the forums promoted an "in-group" status while concurrently targeting "out-groups," an important framework for understanding the *us versus them* mentality (Tajfel & Turner, 1979). This identity theory illustrates how individuals and movements categorize themselves and others into competing social groups, with the in-group sharing a national, racial or religious identity (Berger, 2018). Out-groups of the far-right include, for instance, the Jewish, Muslim and LGBTQIA+ communities; immigrants; black and brown people; left-wing politicians and supporters; the media; and women (Schwarz, 2020). While the far-right may not be a uniform group (Booth, 2023), we believe referring to in- and out-groups is a useful concept in the context of online

---

[2] The term *far-right* here refers to individuals and groups whose ideologies and attitudes are located at the extreme conservative end of the political spectrum (Perliger, 2020), and who hold the belief that violence against their (perceived) enemies is justified (Bjørgo & Ravndal, 2019).

radicalization and how individuals express (dis)alignments with certain people, groups and ideologies.

The technological changes that have enabled a global network of connectivity have also accelerated the radicalization process for a new generation of lone-actor terrorists born into the digital era (Crawford & Keen, 2020; Thorleifsson & Düker 2021). By engaging in online interactions with other extremists in detached webs, subjects appear to feel a sense of unity and commitment to a certain cause (Simi & Windisch, 2020). This has triggered a number of targeted violence attacks that – despite the digital community – are prepared and carried out autonomously. The focal point of this Element, Stephan Balliet, was part of this far-right ecosystem of interchangeable digital platforms where he partly self-radicalized, for instance, on the darknet and clearnet platforms Kohlchan, Nanochan, 8chan, vch.moe and Julay.World (Kupper et al., 2022; Pook, Stanjek & Wigard, 2021). The main research question of this Element is not whether Balliet fits into any specific group, but rather how he constructs an identity as part of *something* – a collection of transnational online extremists with overlapping ideals and connections. By understanding how Balliet aligns with this network, we can gain insights into his ideological frameworks and motives, which ultimately resulted in a violent act of terrorism. This is important as these digital environments where successful lone-actor terrorists with a *high kill count* are glorified (Macklin, 2022) partly inspired Balliet to escape his mundane reality and design a mass casualty incident.

1 Introduction

Disclaimer: Please note that some of the following sections contain graphic language, such as racial slurs and mentions of death and injury.[3] All textual samples were replicated in their original forms, including any kinds of errors.

1.1 The Terrorism Attack

On October 9, 2019, at 11:54 AM, Stephan Balliet is seated in a rental vehicle in a parking lot near a synagogue in the East German town of Halle, Saxony-Anhalt. Intent on conducting a mass shooting at a Jewish place of worship on Yom Kippur – the holiest day in the Jewish calendar – he publishes a link to his targeted violence manifesto (henceforth, TVM) and live-stream on the image-board Meguca at 11:57 AM. After initial technical difficulties when configuring his broadcast to the online gaming platform Twitch, he turns the camera of his phone to his face and announces the following scripted message in English:

---

[3] The main contributor of this section was Julia Kupper.

(1)   Hi my name is Anon,[4] and I think the holocaust never happened. [unintelligible] Feminism is the cause of the decline of birthrates in the West, which acts as a scapegoat for mass immigration. And the root of all these problems is the Jew. Would you like to be friends?

Subsequently, the twenty-seven-year-old German navigates to the synagogue on Humboldtstraße, dressed in a military-style outfit and equipped with a head-mounted phone camera on his ballistic helmet to live-stream his premeditated attack. Antisemitic music is blasting from an MP3 player and loudspeakers attached to the back of a tactical vest (Pook et al., 2021). Balliet arrives at the target site at 12:01 PM and attempts to break into the building – which holds fifty-one worshippers at the time – with homemade explosives, 3D-printed guns and ammunition while broadcasting his attack online to an international audience. Unable to breach the secured doors at the main and side entrances, the perpetrator shoots and fatally wounds a passerby, a forty-year-old female whose only transgression appears to be her vocal complaints about the deafening sounds of the offender's explosives. Visibly agitated, Balliet accidently shoots his car's front tire. When he tries to fire at a second person who has stopped to aid his first victim, Balliet's self-made weapon jams multiple times. Then, the attacker impulsively departs and drives less than 0.3 miles (500 meters), choosing a nearby Turkish restaurant on Ludwig-Wucherer-Straße as a spontaneous second target, and fires shots at several individuals, killing a twenty-year-old male.

The first patrol car arrives at the kebab shop at 12:15 PM – approximately twenty minutes into the incident – and the perpetrator engages in a firefight with several law enforcement officers. Balliet sustains a minor neck injury, drives off, hitting and injuring a Somalian victim walking on the sidewalk, reportedly on purpose. The offender then escapes to the small village of Wiedersdorf, Saxony-Anhalt, nine miles (sixteen kilometers) east of Halle where he attempts to carjack a vehicle at 1:00 PM (Mitteldeutscher Rundfunk, 2019). The car owners, a married couple, refuse to relinquish their vehicle and Balliet shoots and seriously injures them before proceeding to steal a cab to drive towards Munich. Along the way, he discards his phone used to live-stream the attack (Pook et al., 2021). Twenty-five miles (forty kilometers) into his escape, the attacker hits a truck on the freeway and law enforcement apprehends him without further resistance at 1:38 PM (Koehler, 2019). Responding officers discover an escape bag in the vehicle, containing several hygiene and clothing items, as well as food for approximately two days. Balliet explained during his trial that his original plan entailed an escape to the Harz Mountains, a highland area northwest of Halle (Pook et al., 2021).

---

[4] *Anon* is an abbreviation for "anonymous," a username given to profiles in online forums to conceal the user's identity.

Extensive criminal investigations revealed that Balliet carried out the act of terror alone. Over 320 witness interrogations confirmed that there were no indications of contact with groups or individuals that could have assisted the offender with planning and preparing for the targeted attack (Pook et al., 2021). In December 2020, the perpetrator was charged with two counts of murder, seven counts of attempted murder and incitement of the masses, and was sentenced to life imprisonment with subsequent preventative detention (Bundesamt für Verfassungsschutz, 2022).

1.2 The Language Evidence

Minutes before driving to the target location, Balliet announced his intentions in a short message titled *Last Post* on the imageboard Meguca with the help of a wireless internet stick and laptop (Pook et al., 2021). The anime discussion forum was reportedly loosely connected to 4chan and shut down three days after the Halle incident, which resulted in a loss of all forum data (Pook et al., 2021; Thorleifsson & Düker, 2021). During the court proceedings, Balliet stated that it was a *coincidence* that he leaked his materials to this specific website, which seems questionable as the perpetrator planned every other aspect of his targeted act meticulously (Kupper et al., 2022). We believe Balliet chose this particular imageboard because of his interest in anime and gaming (see Sections 3.2 and 4.3) and because 8chan had been taken down after three preceding lone-actor terrorists announced their acts of violence on this platform in March, April and August 2019 (see Sections 7.1 and 8.4).

In the online attack announcement on Meguca, Balliet linked to a folder that contained his TVM, which was authored in English and dissected into three separate files:

- A one-page *READ THIS FIRST* file, which contained a link to the Twitch live-stream and a short message. According to investigations, this document was created on October 1 and edited until four days prior to the incident, October 5, 2019 (Pook et al., 2021).
- An eleven-page *short pre-action report*, comprising photographs and descriptions of his self-manufactured equipment (guns, bullets, grenades), as well as an operational plan and gaming-style objective and achievement sections. The original file name was *dokumentation.pdf*, which translates to "documentation." During the Halle trial, it was stated that Balliet began working on this document on March 26, 2019, eleven days after the New Zealand mosque shooting (March 15, 2019). He continuously added to and edited the file until August 17, 2019, and then picked it up again on September 21, 2019, less than two weeks prior to the attack (Pook et al., 2021).

- A four-page *spiritual guide*, consisting of encouraging statements for others to commit similar attacks and an image of an anime cat-girl. The file name was a Japanese translation of the word "Manifesto." Balliet worked on this document from September 21, 2019, until three days before the attack, October 6, 2019 (Pook et al., 2021).

According to investigation files from Balliet's interrogation conducted by Germany's Federal Criminal Police on November 22, 2019, the assailant claimed to have uploaded all of these communications for *entertainment* purposes (Bundeskriminalamt, 2019).

We also obtained an unreleased self-interview titled *Your F&A Guide* but saved as *Manifest0.pdf* on Balliet's hard drive, which he did not distribute publicly with his other materials. *F&A* is a German abbreviation for "Frage & Antwort," the English equivalent to *Q&A* ("question & answer"). The offender stated that he decided against publishing the file "because it sounded too much like a justification. And only those who do wrong have to justify themselves. And there is nothing wrong with taking action against someone that wants you dead" (Bundeskriminalamt, 2019, p. 2). When asked why the document was authored in English during one of his first police interviews, Balliet responded that he intended to reach a wide audience with it (Pook et al., 2021). Furthermore, the perpetrator explained that he created his *short pre-action report* as a follow-up document to the unreleased self-interview, which was meant to be *a joke* (Bundeskriminalamt, 2019).

The thirty-six-minute recorded live-stream was aired on Twitch, a video-game broadcasting and viewing platform, with Balliet switching between English and German throughout the video that was filmed from a first-person shooter perspective. During his trial, the offender declared that he registered the account *spilljuice* on Twitch a few months before the attack for the sole purpose of streaming his event live (Pook et al., 2021). The phrase *spill juice* is a euphemism for bleeding as a result of a gunshot or stab wound. Balliet opted to use Twitch because Facebook had improved its algorithms to detect and eliminate streams of violent acts quicker after previous terrorism attacks were broadcast on there in 2019. Twitch informed investigators that the original live-stream had a total of three viewers based in the United States and Switzerland, who watched the broadcast for ten, fifteen and thirty minutes each (Pook et al., 2021). By the time the platform identified and deleted Balliet's broadcast, the video had been watched by approximately 2,200 people (Koehler, 2019). Similarly to previous targeted violence live-streams, the recording spread like wildfire online (Kupper et al., 2022).

As a number of scholars have called for multidisciplinary research into threatening language that combines theoretical perspectives from linguistics, rhetoric, psychology and law (Bojsen-Møller, 2021; Gales, 2010 and 2019), we fuse several qualitative methodologies for forensic text analysis and behavioral threat assessment in a novel approach to present a holistic review of the Halle terrorism case. Part one of our interdisciplinary analysis provides a deep dive into Stephan Balliet's targeted violence communications by applying different forensic text assessments to his language evidence, such as genre, text linguistic and appraisal analyses. Part two focuses on the perpetrator's pre-attack behaviors to conduct a retrospective threat assessment and organizational review for security agencies, and incorporates an uptake analysis to highlight the contagion and copycat effect of Balliet's communications and attack.

2 Methodology

2.1 Holistic Review

The objective of this Element is to provide a comprehensive analysis of the language evidence associated with the Halle terrorism attack by conducting a scientific and systematic post-hoc examination of select genre, linguistic and behavioral features.[5] This multi-method approach highlights the need for inter-disciplinary threat assessment teams composed of investigators, psychologists and linguists to tackle various types of evidence and to approach terrorism cases through different lenses. While intelligence analysts can collect and analyze raw data from the digital sphere to identify a potential subject of concern, detectives can conduct search and seizure procedures and interviews to obtain relevant corroborations. This information can then be analyzed by mental health specialists regarding warning behaviors, while linguists can conduct an analysis of written and spoken evidence. Such cross-disciplinary investigations will deepen the understanding of subjects' motivations, ideologies and networks, and thus enhance the ability to determine the level of risk of an impending attack. As TVMs are often disseminated minutes or hours prior to an attack and provide limited time for intervention, our interdisciplinary analysis demonstrates the importance of looking at language corroborations in their wider context as part of an aggregate social act of terrorism. Furthermore, the scientific interest in describing, analyzing and explaining language data in the form of a case study carries great value that can provide a prism through which we can evaluate other cases. Insights gained from retrospective assessments, such as the examination of how warning indicators may have manifested themselves in pre-attack

---

[5] The main contributor of this section was Julia Kupper.

behaviors, contribute to the larger goal of preventing future acts of targeted violence. In concert, the findings assist in enriching our understanding of threat assessment protocols and in devising proactive measures against domestic and foreign threats.

Our analysis first renders a broad overview of the genre of TVMs and of the specific constellation of the TVM that Balliet produced prior to his attack. We then consecutively zoom in on how the language of the TVM relates to the textual and situational context, and on how the language reveals Balliet's stances towards his weapons, his objectives and himself. We then broaden the perspective again to analyze the psychological and behavioral traits that may have caused the attack, and to give an assessment of whether the act of violence could have been prevented through intelligence and investigative measures. Finally, we expand the focus even further to the ramifications in terms of uptakes by other far-right extremists and copycats in different online and offline settings.

This qualitative, multifaceted approach allows us to conduct a critical, in-depth and thorough examination of the perpetrator's communications and actions, and thus provides a comprehensive and nuanced review of the Halle case. All methodologies will be elaborated upon in their respective sections, but here we provide a summary of all manual types of analyses that complement each other to enhance our understanding of the event:

- The *genre analysis* assesses the communicative functions, structure and genre labels of each written communication in the TVM and shows how the perpetrator's self-professed purpose overlaps with and differs from the generic functions of TVMs.
- The *text linguistic analysis* examines the interplay between grammatical, lexical and pragmatic features to reveal the perpetrator's narrative, networks and discursively expressed need for significance.
- The *stance analysis* identifies the assailant's stances through appraisal analysis to provide insights into his motives and ideologies, including his evaluations of the intended targets, his manufactured weapons, his plan and how he presents himself as ideologically (dis)aligned with the audience(s) of his TVM.
- The *retrospective threat assessment* conducts a behavioral analysis of the perpetrator's background, red flags, triggering events and pathway to violence behaviors to accentuate warning indicators that might be utilized to thwart future acts of violence.
- The *organizational review* assesses challenges faced by security authorities when dealing with lone-actor terrorists, including an examination of Balliet's behaviors in the run-up to the crime, to discuss whether information for preventive police measures was available to security authorities.

- The *uptake analysis* examines how the offender's TVM, live-stream and Q&A are a response to – an uptake on – other targeted violence attacks and communications, and how Balliet's actions and words have been taken up by subsequent terrorists and a variety of online communities through different intertextual connections.

2.2 Data Selection and Aggregation

The authors of this Element opted to study Stephan Balliet for several reasons. First, there appears to be a lack of research focusing exclusively on the Halle incident with the exception of a commentary published two months after the attack occurred (Koehler, 2019) and Balliet's TVM and live-stream having been assessed in previous studies (Allchorn, Dafnos & Gentile, 2022; Kupper et al., 2022). Second, far-right terrorism is contemporarily the greatest threat for lone-actor attacks in North America and Europe (Bundesamt für Verfassungsschutz, 2022; Wray, 2021). Third, publicly available data on Balliet was sufficient to apply a multi-method approach to his linguistic corroborations and pre-attack behaviors. The written and spoken evidence compiled by Balliet (i.e., the multi-document TVM, imageboard post and recording of the live-stream) was originally reviewed and analyzed in the days following the attack in the form of an operational analysis when the first author was embedded within a law enforcement agency. All data are also available in the public domain and were subsequently securely stored in an online file system accessible to all authors of this Element. The unpublished file *Your F&A Guide* was later obtained from a private source and only reviewed by the first author to maintain confidentiality. The court trial transcripts were acquired from *democ. Zentrum Demokratischer Widerspruch e.V.*, an association of scientists, journalists and media professionals who jointly observe, document and analyze antidemocratic movements.[6] They transcribed the Halle court proceedings and published their reproduction in Pook et al. (2021).

3 Rhetorical Genre Analysis

In this section, we employ rhetorical genre studies (RGS) to analyze Stephan Balliet's written communications from a genre perspective, showing how they are an enactment of the genre of TVMs.[7] We thus analyze the communicative functions and structure of his TVM and consider how it complies with and diverges from what we know about the overall genre from the literature (Kupper et al., 2022; Kupper & Meloy, 2021). It is also described how Balliet uses genre labels and

---

[6] We thank Grischa Stanjek for providing us with the entire transcripts of the Halle court case.

[7] The main contributor of this section was Marie Bojsen-Møller.

meta-commentary to position himself in regard to his own utterances and their communicative purpose, to the proposed future violent actions that he sketches out in the TVM and to the actual targeted violence act that follows it. Theoretically, this expands our knowledge of the interaction between recurrent aspects of a genre and the individual linguistic manifestation of it. From a practical and societal perspective, it is important to gain a deeper understanding of the TVM genre and Balliet's specific use of it because TVMs are as recurrent an action as the physical act of terrorism itself. It is therefore crucial to know what functions the genre serves and what personal purposes it has for the individual terrorist and thereby understand the multitude of motivations and reasons for the violent actions.

The foundation for the genre analysis is Miller's definition of genres as *typified* (i.e., recurrent) *social actions* (1984) that are manifested through generic types of written or spoken *utterances* (Bakhtin, 1986), for example, greetings, recipes, newspaper articles or threatening communications (Bojsen-Møller et al., 2020). Genres consolidate themselves within certain *discourse communities* (Swales, 2016) and *communities of practice* (Wenger, McDermott & Snyder, 2002) through a mixture of repetition, imitation and innovation.

Within genre theory, there are in essence two approaches to explaining what shapes a genre, that is, what gives it its recognizable interactional, structural and linguistic form. According to Swalesian genre theory, genres are shaped by their *communicative purpose* (Swales, 1990). Within RGS, Miller (2015) instead argues that the term *function* (or *exigence*) is better suited than purpose, since it addresses the shared communicative need from which a genre arises. Purpose refers to the individual point of view of the sender of a specific utterance. In contrast, function refers to a *generalized* point of view and therefore points to the *recurrent social action* (Miller, 1984) that a given genre enacts. We will therefore only use the term communicative *purpose* when referring to Balliet's explicitly stated, self-professed purposes. Conversely, we will use the term *communicative function* when we refer to the generalized function of a text or a genre. The communicative functions of a genre govern the linguistic form of the genre of TVMs (Kupper & Meloy, 2021), and this genre analysis thereby forms the foundation for the linguistic analyses in Sections 4 and 5.

3.1 The Genre of Targeted Violence Manifestos

Kupper and Meloy (2021, p. 6) define the genre of targeted violence manifestos (TVM) as:

> A written or spoken communication intended to justify an act of violence against a specific target by articulating self-identified grievances, homicidal intentions, and/or extreme ideologies for committing an attack. Generally

composed by a single author before the incident occurs, it sometimes expresses beliefs and ideas to violently promote political, religious, or social changes.

Kupper et al. (2022) clarify that TVMs also have the communicative function of inspiring people with like-minded beliefs to commit similar attacks (known as the "contagion and copycat effect," see Section 8.1). In accordance with this, Bakhtin explains that every genre utterance presupposes an inherent *addressivity* (Bakhtin, 1986), that is, an utterance will always have a concept of a sender and an addressee (or audience). Together with communicative functions, the types of senders and addressees are constitutive features of the genre of an utterance.

The typical traits (i.e., communicative functions and addressivity) of a TVM are thus:

- to *announce* and *justify* a future act of intended *violence committed by the author* of the communication prior to their attack;
- to *specify a target* or target group for the attack;
- to *express grievances*, *homicidal plans* and/or *extremist beliefs*;
- to *inspire* other *violent extremists* and possible *future attackers*;
- to *signal in-group membership* to a far-right ecosystem.

Similarly to the genre of threatening communications, TVMs are an *illicit genre* (Bojsen-Møller et al., 2020; Kupper & Meloy, 2021), which are genres that are proscribed by general society. The audiences of illicit genres are typically divided into two distinct groups: supporters and opponents, meaning that illicit genres often have both a desired and an unwanted audience. The desired audience will typically be like-minded in-group members that share the norms of or sympathize with the sender (see Prologue and Sections 4.3, 5.5, 6.3, 7.3 and 8.4). The unwanted audience of illicit genres, the out-group members, will often express condemnation or seek to enforce societal or legal norms upon the sender.

3.2 Communicative Functions, Embedded Genres and Genre Labels

Genres are often embedded within other genres, where each *embedded genre* (Auken, 2021) serves a constituent communicative function that contributes to the total communicative function, for example, a greeting or a thank you can be embedded within a letter and an indictment can be embedded within a record of judgment (Bojsen-Møller, 2022).[8]

---

[8] The concept of embedded genres is comparable to but not identical with Swales' rhetorical *moves* (1990) and Martin's (1994) distinction between *macrogenres and microgenres,* but this will not be discussed further here.

In this case, Balliet made a pre-attack announcement on Meguca.org, linking to a folder and to the Twitch live-stream. The folder contained three PDF files with the file names *READ THIS FIRST*, *dokumentation.pdf* and マニフェスト (Japanese for "Manifesto"). Each of the three documents and their different sections can be considered genres (i.e., typified, communicative social actions) in their own right that are embedded in the overall genre of the TVM. Each embedded genre (each document and each document section in Figure 1) thus serves different, constituent communicative functions, which in combination shape the total communicative functions of the TVM. The genre embeddings reflect the structure of the TVM, as shown in Figure 1.

Balliet uses the names of each PDF file and the headings and subheadings within the files (in short, all titles in italics in Figure 1) to describe and categorize the documents and their distinctive subsections. Titles of texts designate the subject matter of the text, and they function as *thresholds* (Genette, 1997) to the text itself that help guide the reader's interpretation. Titles are identifying devices for the reader, and since they often serve to name the text type itself, they have *genre-indicating properties* (Genette, 1997). Within RGS, such titles – that is, names used to categorize texts – are therefore

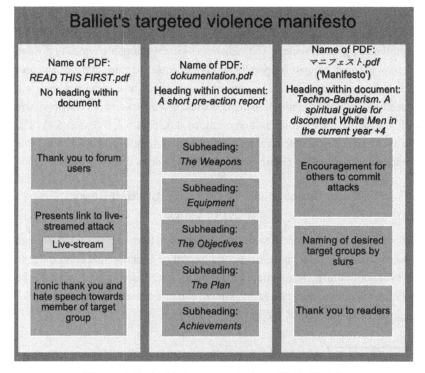

Figure 1 Embedded genres within Balliet's TVM.

called *genre labels* (Nyboe, 2016). Since the genre labels (i.e., the italicized file names, headings and subheadings in Figure 1) that Balliet has chosen for some of the embedded genres in his TVM have a direct bearing on the perceived communicative functions of the texts, the following analysis will consider these genre labels.

3.2.1 The READ THIS FIRST *File*

The genre label (i.e., file name) *READ THIS FIRST* directs the actions of its readers by giving them instructions for their order of reading. It partially replicates the existing genre label "read me first," which is a formulaic title used in technical guidelines to indicate important prerequisites for use. Where "read me first" guidelines usually include technical specifications and factual information, Balliet's *READ THIS FIRST* file rather appears as a preface to the TVM and the live-streamed attack meant for his in-group.

This file thus not only functions as a preface to the two other documents in the TVM but also serves the important communicative function of distributing the link to the live-streamed attack (which will not be analyzed here). Through the genre label *READ THIS FIRST,* Balliet indicates that the live-stream takes precedence over the remaining written documents: The attack itself is the most important part for his audience to watch, whereas the presentation of his cause and ideological convictions can wait. This prioritization of the live-stream is reflected through various intertextual references to it in the TVM. This is in line with Kupper et al., who argue that live-streams of attacks appear to be a "more powerful tool for propaganda than manifestos" (2022, p. 10), since they put the ideals and goals of the theoretical TVMs into violent action.

The *READ THIS FIRST* file also has the dual communicative function of expressing two different types of "thank you" to his expected audiences: He first gives his earnest thank you to his in-group members, writing "Thank you for all the good time anon." Interestingly, *anon* is a reference to anonymous users of fringe message boards, rather than the far-right community (see Section 4.3); a term that Balliet also uses at the beginning of his live-stream (see Section 1.1). Balliet then proceeds to thank one of the members of his target group, calling out "Mark [Mann], former BO [board owner] of 8ch /v/ and owner of vch.moe" (two imageboards for video gamers) who he refers to as a Jewish person. Since we can assume that he does not actually want to thank anyone in his target group, this must be seen as an ironic thank you. It is thus an example of humor being used negatively as a way of denigrating the target of the humorous utterance, which is a typical use of humor that is often seen in far-right communities (Fielitz & Ahmed, 2021; Norrick, 2010; see Sections 4.3 and 5.6).

3.2.2 The dokumentation.pdf *File*

The second document in Figure 1, with the file name *dokumentation.pdf* and the within-text heading *A short pre-action report*, is the most substantive document in the TVM in terms of length and topics covered. The genre labels *dokumentation* and *A short pre-action report* point to the primary communicative functions of the report, namely that of documenting the planning stages before the attack itself (the *action*). The genre label *A short pre-action report* implies that even though this may be the main part of the written TVM, it is merely secondary to the *action* itself – to the live-streamed attack. The genre of "report" usually refers to a detailed description of an event or situation, often conducted by someone in an official capacity. Combined with the fact that presenting the weapons and equipment is the main focus of the *short pre-action report*, this genre label gives the document an aura of military professionalism that is perhaps a welcome connotation for its author.

In what follows, we dive deeper into the *short pre-action report* and the communicative functions of its constituent sections. Table 1 shows the embedded genres, as labeled by Balliet, and their contents.

The Weapons Section

The first section, labeled *The Weapons*, constitutes the main part of the *short pre-action report*, being by far the longest and most detailed section. As indicated by the genre label of the heading, this section presents and assesses the weapons Balliet designed and built through pictures and descriptions. Kupper et al. (2022) list visual displays of weapons on online platforms, but not in the TVMs themselves, as a typical trait in cases concerning targeted violence offenders. Balliet's extreme emphasis on showcasing his weapons is not typical of other TVMs, except for Payton Gendron,[9] who mirrored Balliet's

Table 1 Genre embedding, structure and content of the *short pre-action report*

Section Headings	Content
The Weapons, pages 1–9	Presentation and assessment of weapons
Equipment, page 9	Presentation and assessment of other equipment
The Objectives, page 9	List of goals in committing the violent attack
The Plan, page 10	Critical assessment of his plans and justification of the chosen target group
Achievements, page 11	Gaming-type list of achievements

---

[9] A lone-actor terrorist who committed an attack at a supermarket in Buffalo, New York, in May 2022.

weapons section in his TVM (see Section 8.4). Another feature that diverges from the typical communicative functions of TVMs is that Balliet expresses serious doubts concerning the success of his plans and the reliability of his self-made guns (see Sections 4.4 and 5.1). Norris (2024) reports that some attackers do express hesitations or doubts regarding the success of their plans and the possibility of those plans not succeeding in their TVMs, but not to the extent that we see in Balliet's TVM. Nonetheless, the *Weapons* section does reflect one of the typical communicative functions of TVMs (see Section 3.1), namely that of articulating homicidal intentions against a target. In (2), we see this in reference to a homemade pistol:

(2)   Protection against getting interrupted while reloading or clearing a malfunction. Can be used to finish of injured foes

Balliet here reflects on different strategies that he intends to follow in his attack, including which weapons may be most effective. The *foes* or enemies are only mentioned fleetingly in the *Weapons* section, thus again underlining the fact that Balliet is mostly concentrated on presenting his weapons and not on his target(s).

The Equipment Section

The *Equipment* section is very short compared to other sections and, in accordance with its genre label, mostly includes a description of the remaining equipment to be used in the attack. Balliet's explicitly stated (see (3)) primary purposes of presenting his weapons and equipment and relaying his experience with constructing and testing the firearms are again evident in this segment. The importance of the live-stream is also noticeable in the *Equipment* section, as he references the filming equipment that he intends to use during the attack.

The Objectives Section

As indicated by the genre label, the section labeled *The Objectives* in the *short pre-action report* has the communicative function of offering Balliet's personal objectives or purposes for committing the attack:

(3)   1. *Prove the viability of improvised weapons.*
        2. *Increase the moral of other suppressed Whites by spreading the combat footage.*
        3. *Kill as many anti-Whites as possible, jews preferred.*
        Bonus: Don't die.

Balliet explicitly asserts his primary purpose in writing the TVM and performing the attack, which is to show off his self-made weapons. As mentioned previously, this is not one of the typical communicative functions of a TVM, and it is therefore a noteworthy divergence from the genre (see Sections 4.4, 5.1, 6.3 and 7.3). In the second objective, to increase the morale of *other suppressed Whites*, he designates his desired audiences; those that may be inspired by him and become copycats (see Section 8.4). This self-professed purpose is in line with the typical communicative functions of a TVM. As the third objective, he defines who his selected target group is to be, namely *anti-Whites* but *jews preferred* (see Section 4.2). This is also one of the typical communicative functions of a TVM, but Balliet describes his preferred target group in very general terms and no specific personal grievances are identified. Perhaps unsurprisingly, there are no indications of empathy with his targets or of a guilty conscience (see Section 6.3). The target is presented as merely a tertiary objective for him, whereas showcasing his weapons and inspiring his desired uptake community are his primary ones.

The Plan Section

The genre label of the *Plan* section raises an expectation that this segment will include an outline of Balliet's plan for the attack. However, it primarily presents an explanation of why he decided on the synagogue as his target; a largely negative assessment of whether his plans will succeed or not (see Sections 4.2 and 5.3); as well as speculations about the different alternatives he might have to succeed. The self-professed *conclusion* of his plan is said to be decided *on site* when the attack is to take place, thus underlining that his attack is not tied to a particular plan.

The main communicative function of the *Plan* section is to offer instructions for those of his readers who wish to perform similar acts of violence, but in addition, Balliet downplays expectations for the success of his plan. He does this in a way that appears to cater to readers who crave entertainment, namely through self-deprecating comic relief (4):

(4)   Oh, and on top of THAT I have not the slightest clue how the floor plan looks like. Intel is the most important aspect of an operation and my capabilities are rather limited.

Throughout the TVM, Balliet uses such self-deprecating humor in what seems like an attempt to connect with his in-group. Humor is often used to *build camaraderie* (Norrick, 2010) for senders to align themselves with their preferred audience (Bojsen-Møller, 2023). Since one of Balliet's self-professed communicative purposes is to inspire members of his in-group to commit similar attacks, the expressions of disparagement against his plans may also be taken as a way of countering later criticism or ridicule by his peers, in case something goes wrong during the event itself (which it did; see Section 1.1).

At the end of the *Plan* section, Balliet shows his powerful resolve in committing the attack and his general antagonism against Jewish people, see (5):

(5)   If I fail and die but kill a single jew, it was worth it.

Articulating such homicidal intentions against a target are typical genre traits in TVMs (Kupper & Meloy, 2021) and can be seen as an obligatory feature of a TVM and thereby a genre-constitutive trait (see Section 3.1).

The Achievements Section

In the *Achievements* section, Balliet presents a list of aspirational accomplishments for the attack, consisting of sardonic wordplays between sets of sentences and phrases. The genre label *Achievements* is well-known within video gaming, and Balliet composed his list to mirror the structure and tone of this genre. As such, it contains a number of objectives that the "player" can strive towards unlocking during his "gameplay" (see Section 4.3). One of the communicative functions of titles is enticement for prospective readers (Genette, 1997), and the connotations of this particular genre label will probably only be recognized by members of gaming communities. The genre label and the compositional frame of this segment thus carry the implication that the communicative function of the *Achievements* section is to bond with and inspire an in-group that also know these references. Furthermore, the use of humor as a communicative strategy to bond with his in-group is particularly evident in this part of the TVM (see Section 4.3). One of the achievements addresses his in-group of expert computer users, see (6):

(6)   *Hello World!*
        Have a successful live-stream.

The headline consists of the greeting *Hello World!* which highlights the intertextual nature of most of his writing. "Hello, World" is established as a stock phrase in computer programming since it forms part of a simple line of programming used to train beginners in many programming languages. The imperative clause references the live-stream that Balliet broadcasted on Twitch and which he links to in his announcement and in the *READ THIS FIRST* file. In total, the greeting exemplifies Balliet's continual appeals to his audience, a feature that permeates the TVM and gives a dialogic flavor to a necessarily monologic document. However, in (6), he is not merely focusing on his in-group members but on all possible readers and viewers. He here shows an understanding of the fact that his live-stream, his TVM and his violent attack will make him known – infamous – to the *world* and not just within his in-group community.

3.2.3 The マニフェスト ("Manifesto") File

If the *READ THIS FIRST* document functions as a preface to the TVM, the document with the file name マニフェスト would function as an epilogue or a postscript. As mentioned previously, マニフェスト is Japanese for "manifesto," that is, the typical genre label for a TVM (henceforth referred to as "Manifesto").

If the "Manifesto" genre label is taken literally, this document would then in fact be the main document of the TVM – or rather, it would be the *entire* TVM – and the *READ THIS FIRST* document and the *short pre-action report* would instead both be prefaces to the real TVM. The "Manifesto" does in fact fulfill several of the communicative functions of TVMs (see Section 3.1), which would substantiate that claim. The communicative function of the text is delimited through the genre label used as a heading within the document *Techno-Barbarism. A spiritual guide for discontent White Men in the current year +4*,[10] that is, to incite other white supremacists to commit similar attacks, as we see throughout his uploaded files. He encourages them to become "Techno-Barbarians," which are brutal warriors within the fantasy war game Warhammer 40K. Techno-Barbarians in Warhammer are equipped with a mixture of primitive and technically advanced weapons and equipment, and it is therefore no surprise that he finds inspiration in these fantasy figures, considering his fixation on self-made weapons. Aside from such attempts to recruit prospective violent offenders through references to shared insider knowledge, the "Manifesto" file also comprises hateful, racist slurs against different target groups, further manifesting typical genre traits of TVMs.

Balliet's choice to write the name of the file in Japanese is consonant with the fact that the files were uploaded to an anime discussion forum on the imageboard Meguca.org ("anime" is a Japanese style of animation). Other Japanese references are found within the document in the form of a picture of an anime cat-girl, which Balliet, in the style of an advertisement, promises as a prize for the readers who commit similar attacks (to become Techno-Barbarians). The anime cat-girl accentuates Balliet's mixture of dark humor and internet culture against the heavy severity of his hate speech towards the groups he aims to harm (see Sections 4.2 and 4.3). The ominous implications of the Japanese genre label will be lost on people who either do not know or take an interest in Japanese (or who do not translate the title) but will conversely entice readers who are part of the Japanese-inspired anime culture on Meguca. Even if the readers on Meguca could not immediately decipher the meaning of it, the Japanese title may have attracted more readers who have a broad interest in Japanese culture. Through this genre label, Balliet has further designated his desired uptake community, namely the online communities surrounding imageboards such as Meguca or "the chans,"

---

[10] This is a reference to the influx of refugees and migrants to Germany in 2015–2016.

where recruitment of prospective targeted violence offenders may occur (Dittrich et al., 2022; Scrivens et al., 2021; see Section 8.4).

3.3 Conclusion

In this section, we have demonstrated how an RGS approach can outline the communicative functions as well as the self-professed communicative purposes of a specific TVM. We have also identified how these communicative functions and purposes diverge from and converge with the typical traits of the genre of TVMs. We have thereby sought to gain a deeper understanding of the complex motivations behind TVMs and targeted violence attacks.

Throughout the TVM, Balliet uses genre labels to guide his readers and introduce the content of the documents. The various genre labels reflect the primary communicative functions of his TVM, which are: (1) to showcase his self-made weapons and to document the attack, and (2) to address the far-right community and encourage future violent attackers.

Balliet's documents are an enactment of the genre of TVMs, as they constitute an announcement of his later targeted violence attack against a specific target, that is, the Jewish synagogue and thereby the Jewish community. However, the perpetrator's self-professed communicative purposes deviate from the typical function of a TVM by prioritizing the presentation of his improvised weapons over relaying extremist ideologies or justifying the violent attack.

In the next two sections, we zoom in on the language of the Halle TVM to provide more texture and detail to the analysis. In Section 4, we show how a text linguistic analysis can uncover not only the underlying ideological narrative for the attack but also the perpetrator's complex online networks and his need for significance.

4 Text Linguistic Analysis

4.1 The Role of Context

This section offers a text linguistic analysis of the Halle TVM, adducing three sources of information to deepen our insight into this text and its role in the attack: (1) the communicative functions outlined in the previous section, (2) the linguistically signaled connections within the text, and (3) the lexical and social meanings that allow for a reconstruction of the situational context.[11] When analyzing nonfictional texts, situational context is integral to the interpretation of utterance meaning. In criminal cases, however, contextual information may be quite limited, reducing the interpretive potential of pragmatic analyses, such as

---

[11] The main contributor of this section was Tanya Karoli Christensen.

the analysis of indirect speech acts (Searle, 1979) and implicatures (Grice, 1975). Even absent such contextual information, the surrounding text forms a *textual context* for words and utterances, and, here, text linguistic analyses can provide a richer and more detailed understanding of both explicit and implicit meanings.

Text linguistics refers to the study of linguistic structure and meaning in longer stretches of written or spoken language, that is, "texts" (De Beaugrande & Dressler, 1981; Halliday & Webster, 2014), and the approach resembles at least some versions of discourse analysis (Shuy, 2015; Vagle & Wikberg, 2001; van Dijk, 1977). Text linguistic analysis places a particular focus on cohesive devices, such as pronouns and connectors (i.e., conjunctions and linking adverbs, also called (con)junctives; De Beaugrande & Dressler, 1981; Halliday & Hasan 2014 [1976]). In addition, it typically includes a pragmatic element in seeking to resolve semantic ambiguities and presuppositions (Levinson, 1983), and analyzing speech acts and implicatures. All levels of language contribute to a text's *textuality* (De Beaugrande & Dressler, 1981), and while a text linguistic analysis can proceed chronologically – from beginning to end – such a procedure quickly becomes unmanageable for longer texts. We find that a better approach is to structure the analysis around topics of relevance to the genre at hand or to the text's unique features. Here, we draw inspiration from the notion of a *quest for significance*, which has been proposed as the underlying motivation for different types of violent extremists (Kruglanski et al., 2018) and use its component elements to structure our analysis.

4.1.1 Analytic Topics: Need, Narrative and Network

The Significance Quest Theory outlined by Kruglanski et al. (2018) argues that a person who has experienced a severe loss of significance in their life "is more likely to choose violent extremism if he or she encounters an ideological narrative portraying violence as a viable antidote to insignificance, and/or a social network that advances this narrative within their social milieu" (Kruglanski et al., 2018, p. 109, emphasis added; see Section 6.3 on how Balliet's illness was the catalyst of his social withdrawal and thwarting of occupational goals). These people adopt an ideological narrative, which on the one hand blames an enemy for their perceived loss, and on the other hand affords them a path to regained significance through violence and self-sacrifice. In other words, the need for significance can be fulfilled by harming an out-group for the good of the in-group (see Tajfel & Turner, 1979), in the Halle case, respectively, the Jewish community and the far-right.

Since the narratives of the far-right are key components in how lone-actor terrorist attacks influenced by these sentiments are planned and justified, we begin this text linguistic analysis by highlighting how Balliet's TVM presents and presupposes the conspiracy theory of population replacement. On this background, we examine the networks (or in-group communities) evidenced in Balliet's use of jargon-like lexicon, and how his positioning within these networks affects the way he seeks to gain significance.

4.2 The Narrative

As detailed in Section 3.1, TVMs have several communicative functions, amongst them the justification of violence, the targeting of particular victims and the expression of grievances and extremist beliefs. Throughout his multi-document TVM, Balliet demonstrates his adherence to the far-right conspiracy theory termed the *Great Replacement* or *White Genocide*, according to which white people are being supplanted from their home countries by an obscure Jewish cabal that controls Western governments (Bracke & Hernández Aguilar, 2023; see Sections 5.2, 6.3, 7.2 and 8.4). As Bartlett and Miller (2010, p. 31) note, "the greater the conspiracy, the greater the act required" to awaken people to its existence. Thus, believers in population replacement theories consider lethal violence justified, both to counter the effects of the conspiracy and to recruit new members (see Section 8.4).

Balliet's list of *Objectives* in the *short pre-action report* (see Section 3.2) contains two items that reference such far-right conspiracy theories, see (7)–(8), repeated from (3):

(7)   Increase the moral of other suppressed Whites by spreading the combat footage.

(8)   Kill as many anti-Whites as possible, jews preferred.

The noun phrase *other suppressed Whites* in (7) triggers two presuppositions (Levinson, 1983), namely that (some) white people are being repressed by society and that Balliet is part of that group. According to the objective in (8), the remedy to this maltreatment is to murder those who are opposed to white people (the selection of the prefix *anti-* instead of *non-* signals that Balliet refers to a stance, not a skin color). Further, there is social meaning in the reversal of conventional practices of capitalization in *anti-Whites* and *jews* (Sebba, 2012). The juxtaposition of the two group names shows the deviation from orthographical norms to be deliberate and thereby performative of an underlying ideology (Bucholtz & Hall, 2005). Capitalizing *White* performs a sociocultural elevation of white people over all other groups; in other words, Balliet's nonstandard spelling can be considered a typographical instance of white supremacy and hate speech (ECRI, 2016).

Linguistically, it is worth noting the use of imperatives throughout the *Objectives* list. Imperative clauses belong to the class of speech acts called directives, that is, speech acts that request or instruct the addressee to perform a certain action (Searle,

2008 [1965]). Written in a TVM, the person expected to perform these actions is Balliet himself, and in this sense, the objectives have the indirect speech act force of commissives (committing the sender to these actions). Being formed without a grammatical subject, imperatives omit explicit reference to an agent, which allows them to be easily lifted out of their original context and inserted into new ones (Briggs & Bauman, 1990). Phrasing the objectives as imperative clauses thus facilitates the dissemination of far-right messages in wider forums.

The subsequent section of the *short pre-action report*, called the *Plan*, contains several other explicit and implicit references to the conspiratorial narrative (Baele, 2019) to which Balliet subscribes. From the very beginning, the target is designated as a Jewish place of worship; see (9):

(9)   First there is the local synagogue. Damn, that's not a soft target.

The wording of the first sentence in (9) has text linguistic significance, since the initial adverbial *First* is a connector signifying that at least one other element should be listed. In this text, however, it is never followed up with a continuation. This incomplete list structure indicates an unfinished train of thought, which may furthermore reveal that Balliet considered alternative targets. By analyzing his use of connectors further down on the same page, we can reconstruct his thinking and how it relates to the narrative: In a paragraph near the end of the *Plan*, Balliet explains his reasoning in selecting this target over other, perhaps more opportune, targets; see (10):

(10)   I originally planned to storm a mosque or an antifa "culture" center, which are way less defended, but even killing 100 golems won't make a difference, when on a single day more than that are shipped to Europe.

The temporal connector *originally* implies that Balliet's plans have changed. At first, he had two possible targets, the Muslim community and members of Antifa, presented as equally desirable through the coordinating connector *or*. This reflects far-right thinking in that Muslims are considered "non-white" (and thereby part of the population replacement conspiracy) and Antifa are characterized as *traitors* (Baele, 2019; Finley & Esposito, 2020). Following up on the implication of changed plans, the next main clause is introduced by the disjunctive connector *but*, which here indicates that there is a disconnect between the original plan and the desired outcome. Further, Balliet deploys a term from Jewish folklore, the *golem*, a concept that has been adopted in popular culture to refer to a humanoid entity controlled by a master (Golem, 2023). Given the narrative, the master lurking in the background is the aforementioned Jewish cabal. This interpretation is supported by the presuppositions triggered by the phrase *shipped to*, which relies on assumptions that the people in question originate outside of their planned destination (here Europe) and that someone else controls their transport as if they were cargo freight (a metaphor that contributes to the far-right dehumanization of immigrants).

The subsequent sentence to (10) affirms this analysis; see (11) and its continuation quoted in (5):

(11)   The only way to win is to cut of the head of ZOG [. . .]

The acronym *ZOG* stands for the "Zionist Occupation Government," a cardinal antagonist of far-right conspiracy theories and typically integrated into the population replacement narrative (Bartlett & Miller, 2010; Bergmann, 2018). The noun phrase *The only way* presupposes that some might believe there are other options and simultaneously denies this possibility, representing a kind of fatalistic thinking characteristic of the far-right.

4.3 The Networks

Since one of the communicative functions of a TVM is to incite followers to conduct further attacks, we would expect Balliet's network to consist of other far-right extremists. However, the text linguistic analysis reveals that this is not the full picture. From the lexicon used in the documents, we can see that he also belongs to at least two other communities, namely constructors of homemade weapons and an amalgamation of "extremely online" internet users (in practice, information-sharing activists, gamers, anime fans and memers; see Section 3.2).

Based on the desire to perform violent attacks, it is not surprising that a far-right extremist such as Balliet is interested in weapons. However, in the *Weapons* section of the *short pre-action report*, he directly addresses a specific audience, namely those with limited access to commercial weapons; see (12):

(12)   After all some of you fellows don't have the luxury of industrial-made equipment.

The expression *some of you fellows* implies that he is not himself part of this group, and we do see in the *Weapons* section that he owns a few professional firearms. Nonetheless, the majority of his weapons are homemade. In offering detailed instructions on how to construct homemade firearms and explosives, Balliet simultaneously aligns himself with the far-right agenda of committing mass-shooting attacks and with a group of potential perpetrators who live in regions with strict gun regulations.

In a separate document of the TVM, the *READ THIS FIRST* file, we see a reflection of the transnational networks when Balliet first references US currency (*50$*) – and note how he employs the European convention of placing the currency marker after the amount – and then uses metric measurements (*5g*) in the same sentence; see (13):

(13)   All you need is a weekend worth of time and <u>50$</u> for the materials. Cartridges can
        be made from paper, primers can be made from match heads, <u>5g</u> black powder is
        an efficient main charge.

The second-person pronoun *you* can be either read generically or as a deictic
reference to his intended audience, that is, those who wish to construct their own
weapons (see Section 3.2).

As mentioned, Balliet's TVM also shows his connections with other communities or networks, especially ones in the online sphere (see Sections 3.2 and 7.3).
Throughout the documents, Balliet uses jargon that evidences his deep engagement
with both fringe and mainstream internet culture such as file-sharing activists
(Bauer et al., 2009), videogaming (Squire, 2014), meme culture (Kostadinovska-
Stojchevska & Shalevska, 2018) and anime fandom (Ray et al., 2017). We begin by
listing some examples of this in-group lexicon, organized by the domains they refer
to (all can be looked up online, e.g., on the website *Know Your Meme:* https://
knowyourmeme.com/memes/).

- File-sharing activism
  - *seeding:* digital file sharing through decentralized, peer-to-peer computer
    networks (pre-attack announcement)
  - *magnet link:* hyperlink for downloading data in peer-to-peer networks
    (pre-attack announcement)

- Gaming
  - *8ch /v/:* a sub-board on 8chan on videogaming (*READ THIS FIRST*)
  - *vch.moe:* a now defunct videogaming imageboard (*READ THIS FIRST*)
  - *Achievements:* meta-goals in video games (*short pre-action report*)
  - *Techno-Barbarian:* a class of warriors from the table-top and video game
    Warhammer ("Manifesto")

- Internet and meme culture
  - *shitpost:* deliberately provocative and derailing comments online (*short
    pre-action report*)
  - *jej:* a (perhaps once typo-induced) version of *LOL*, "laughing out loud"
    (*short pre-action report*)
  - *Tldr:* abbreviation of "too long; didn't read," used to headline a short
    summary (*short pre-action report*)
  - Headlines of several of the *Achievements* (*short pre-action report*), for
    example,
    - *Think of the children:* meme from the animated sit-com *The Simpsons*
    - *Why not both?:* meme from an old taco commercial
    - *The fire rises:* quote from the Batman movie *The Dark Knight Rises*

- *If I only had one bullet ...* partial quote from Romanian antisemitic Cornelia Codreanu's book *For my Legionaries*
- *This is my BOOM-STICK:* quote from the fantasy comedy *Army of Darkness*, part of The Evil Dead series.
- *The Eternal Anglo:* anti-British meme coined after the antisemitic expression "The Eternal Jew"

- Anime
  - *weeb:* a person who likes anime and Japanese culture (*short pre-action report*)
  - *waifu:* Japanese transliteration of English *wife*, an attractive fictional female (*short pre-action report*; "Manifesto")
  - *cat-girl:* an anime/manga hybrid of a cat and a woman ("Manifesto")

These phrases not only demonstrate Balliet's proficiency in internet vernacular but also place him in a complex network of partially overlapping communities, whose combination serves to circumscribe the perpetrator's online world. Most of these communities are not extremists, but the far-right has been shown to infiltrate some of the online networks to recruit new members, in particular through the use of humor (see Prologue and Sections 3.2 and 5.6).

To illustrate the way Balliet combines lexicon from all these spheres, we zoom in on two excerpts from the *short pre-action report*. First, one of the *Achievements*, see (14):

(14) *Blue-screened*
      Kill a ZOG-bot.

Blue-screened signifies the blue-colored screen shown after a system crash on the Windows operating system. In this context, it is extended metaphorically to cover the death of a victim, here referenced as a *ZOG-bot*. In computer terminology, a *bot* is a software application built to communicate with users, but since Balliet is planning a live event, it is likely meant as a derogatory term for someone who mindlessly follows their master's directions (see the term *golem*). In using the compound *ZOG-bot*, Balliet thus signals to both his far-right network and a collective of computer savvy internet citizens. Secondly, the final paragraph of *the Plan* forms a short summary of Balliet's plan of action; see (15):

(15) Tldr:
      Choose the best way for entry spontaneous. Go in and kill everything.
      Improvise, if when something goes wrong. Drive away. Kill some more.
      Repeat until all jews are dead or you prove the existence of Waifus in Valhalla, whatever comes first. Jej.

This excerpt evidences Balliet's embedding in internet culture through his use of the abbreviations *Tldr* and *jej* (see the list of in-group jargon terms), strikethrough (~~if~~ *when*) as a humorous indication of self-correcting (see also Section 5.1), and the cross-cultural terms *Waifus* and *Valhalla*. This latter combination identifies Balliet as belonging not just to the wider network of anime fans but to a narrower group who are also white supremacists. *Valhalla* is a term from Norse mythology designating the glorified hall of warriors in Asgard, the realm of the gods. A subset of contemporary followers of Norse mythology (Ásatrú) is "overtly white supremacist, claiming that Ásatrú is the true religion of the superior 'Aryan race'" (Weber, 2018). As summarized by Koehler (2019, p. 15) in an early study of the Halle attack, "[t]he mixture of Japanese anime culture with Norse mythology is striking and is reminiscent of jihadi promises of 72 virgins awaiting the martyr in paradise."

However, other parts of the *short pre-action report* indicate that Balliet did not seek to achieve martyrdom in the form of death (although he may have sought "sainthood" for his actions, see Sections 6.3, 7.2 and 8.4); see (16) and (17):

(16)   Bonus: Don't die

(17)   there's quite the possibility that I fail to get in and instead spill my spaghetti all over the street [...] I would rather prefer to not do that.

Both of these excerpts suggest that this offender may have sought the death of his victims, but not of himself. This leads us to the "need for significance" and how Balliet tailored this to his personal goals.

4.4 The Need

As mentioned in Section 3.2, Balliet's TVM distinguishes itself from other far-right TVMs in prioritizing weapons testing over targeting certain victim groups and inspiring other attackers. This appears not only in the *Objectives* list in the *short pre-action report* but also in the body of the *Weapons* section; see (18):

(18)   the whole deal is to show the viability of improvised guns.

The fixed expression *the whole deal* in (18) means "the point of it all" and we can infer that Balliet is referring to the point of the planned attack. Paradoxically, merely raising the question of the weapons' *viability* invites the implicature that they may not in fact function as well as desired (Grice, 1975). At the same time, the technical vocabulary used in the *Weapons* section demonstrates an intense personal interest in mastering the construction of homemade weapons. This reveals that Balliet seeks to gain significance by overcoming one of the obstacles for escalating mass casualty attacks transnationally, namely the restricted access to firearms and ammunition. By providing future attackers with a blueprint to construct their own weapons, it matters less to Balliet whether his own attack is successful and more that his knowledge about weapons assembly is disseminated (see also Sections 3.2, 5.1, 6.3 and 7.3).

Similarly, some of the gaming-style *Achievements* indicate a resignation to possible defeat, which to some extent contrasts with the notions of heroic martyrdom (*Valhalla*) and therefore with the violent extremist *quest for significance* (Kruglanski et al., 2018; but see Sections 6.3, 7.2 and 8.4 on how he may still have sought "sainthood"). While most of the achievements contain violent verbs (primarily *kill*) and can be considered *pledges-to-harm* (Hurt, 2020), the list is bookended by two achievements that simultaneously reflect a determination to execute the plan and a concern for the consequences. The first achievement iconically refers to the first step of Balliet's plan; see (19):

(19)   *No way back.*
       Upload this PDF.

The expression *No way back* is used in a figurative sense to indicate that a course of action has proceeded too far to be aborted and typically implies a risk of regret. In distinction to most of the other achievements, which are all generic and could take anyone as the agent of the designated action, the imperative phrase in (19) contains a deictic reference to the TVM itself: *this PDF* must refer to Balliet's own TVM and it thus directly implicates himself. Uploading, and thereby broadcasting, the TVM counts as the first step in a performative speech act for Balliet, since he in effect declares "I hereby commit myself to this pledge-to-harm" (Hurt, 2020). Making the documents available online puts him in touch with recipients who would have otherwise been oblivious to his plans. It is only in establishing (the preconditions for) this contact that the speech act begins to have social consequences; if there were no recipients to acknowledge the commissive speech act, it would not function as a performative. But as soon as the performative act is accomplished, Balliet is enmeshed in a powerful interactional bond that forces him to continue with his plan, however vaguely defined it is (notably, Germany is one of the jurisdictions in which the act of uploading a TVM is a criminal offense in itself, since it shows intent to carry out a violent attack). It is therefore no trivial matter that Balliet begins by broadcasting his intentions; on the contrary, this communicative act demonstrates his need for significance.

The final achievement focuses more directly on the risk of harm to himself; see (20):

(20)   *I liked that hand* ...
       Accidentally frag yourself
       with the improvised explosives.

This achievement is unique in this list by containing deictically referring personal pronouns, conventionally pointing to the author (the first-person pronoun *I*) and the reader (the reflexive second-person pronoun *yourself*). Both will pragmatically refer to the person who takes up the challenge (in the first run: Balliet), who then can project themselves simultaneously into the semantic roles of agent (*I*) and patient (*yourself*) of this action. The simple past *liked* invites the implicature that the object in question (the hand) is no longer in the person's possession and that this state of affairs is regrettable. Taken together with the imperative clause and the adverbial *Accidentally*, this achievement thus places the responsibility for losing a hand on the offender himself. The shift between first- and second-person pronouns is indicative of a split perspective on the action from the inside and the outside, as well as from the immediate and the later future (from where one can look back upon the unfortunate consequences of prior actions). While this last of the achievements does align with the commitment of the rest, it also reveals a lack of confidence in his abilities to successfully carry through the attack, and thus contributes to the self-degrading intonation of the entire TVM. At the same time, the TVM has a humorous tone, which seems intended to offset the overall despondency (also see Section 3.2). This shows that Balliet's need for significance lies just as much in gaining acknowledgement from his network(s) as in fighting against the purported "population replacement."

4.5 Conclusion

In this section, we have shown how a text linguistic analysis can explicate the underlying meanings in the language of a TVM to reveal the offender's narrative, networks and need for significance. The analysis of Balliet's narrative showed that it aligns with white supremacist population replacement conspiracy theories. The analysis of his networks found that his language displays a strong affiliation with the "extremely online" internet culture, and in particular with the gaming, anime and illicit file-sharing communities. While the gamification of offline behavior does not indicate radicalization, it is an established fact that the extreme right uses gaming forums online to identify possible new recruits (see Prologue and Fizek & Dippel, 2020). Finally, in the analysis of Balliet's need for significance, we argue that he tailors his quest to his individual interests and objectives by leveraging his expertise in weapons construction and internet vernacular to gain acknowledgement from his peers. For one, his action objectives appear strategic rather than tactical in the sense that a successful deployment of his homemade firearms and explosives would pave the way for other extremists to construct their own weapons and thereby circumvent the difficulties in obtaining professional guns. Secondly, the effort put into crafting amusing and memetic expressions throughout the TVM shows how important the tone of Balliet's communications were to his attempt to position himself relative to his networks.

The following section delves deeper into Balliet's affiliation with the far-right and how it manifests through interpersonal stances in his *short pre-action report*.

5 Stance Analysis

Stance, or a person's expressed "personal feelings, attitudes, value judgments, or assessments about a theme, recipient or proposition" (Gales, 2021, p. 675; see Biber et al., 1999) has been a focal point in studies relating to social identity and relationships (Kiesling, 2009; Ochs, 1992).[12] Recent research, particularly on texts by violent actors (e.g., Etaywe & Zappavigna, 2023; Gales, 2010; Hunter & Grant, 2022; Wing, 2017), suggests that understanding authorial stances can offer important insights into assailants' expressed positioning of themselves and others, with aims of identifying discursively encoded motivating factors and ideological (dis)alignments. Examining stances in Balliet's TVM may provide insights into his motives and ideologies, shedding light on the relationships with his intended targets (out-group) and the ideal audience (in-group), demonstrating his discursive positioning as part of the far-right.

Grounded in systemic functional linguistics (Halliday, 1978), appraisal analysis (Martin & White, 2005) provides a framework for interpreting language use as a result of the interplay between its systematicity and its functionality. Building off the insights from Sections 3 and 4, this section employs appraisal analysis to examine authorial stances in the *short pre-action report* of Balliet's TVM.

These stances are represented in three interconnected systems: *Attitude*, *Engagement* and *Graduation*. Together, these allow for a system that "permit[s] us to move beyond intuitive, ideologically based assessments of the function of language" (Gales, 2011, p. 30).[13]

1. *Attitude* relates to how feelings are encoded through *affect* (emotions), *judgment* (ethics and esteem), *appreciation* (aesthetics) and *inclination* (desire and fears).
2. *Engagement* refers to how the author positions themself relative to past/future audiences and dialogic voices,[14] which can be *monoglossic* (referring to no other viewpoints) or *heteroglossic* (referring to other voices or recognizing

---

[12] The main contributor of this section was Dakota Wing.
[13] See Martin and White (2005) for a full description of Appraisal Analysis, and Gales (2021) for a practical guide for applying it in forensic contexts.
[14] See Sections 3.1 and 8.2 for a description of Bakhtin's (1986) notion of dialogism.

alternative positions). *Heteroglossic* utterances can be expansive (allow other voices to participate) or contractive (close off the floor to debate).

3. *Graduation* relates to how utterances are *intensified* (upscaled) or *mitigated* (downscaled).

The initial coding revealed patterned appraised items that largely reflect the sections of the *short pre-action report* (see Table 1). As such, we find it useful to present the analysis organized by appraised items. Doing so permits this analysis to be centered around what Balliet is reacting to, or what things are *triggering* his emotions (Martin & White, 2005). The appraised items include:

- Weapons and equipment
- Targets
- Plans
- Goals (objectives and achievements)
- Ideal audience (the far-right community)
- Himself

Appraisal analysis has been shown to be a useful tool in identifying linguistic manifestations of authorial intent (Gales, 2011; Hurt, 2020) and we demonstrate its utility in what follows by revealing patterned stances in Balliet's TVM with a discursive positioning as part of the far-right. These insights are taken up in Sections 6.3 and 9.1 in discussing the psychology behind his actions and the importance for threat assessment.

5.1 Evaluations of Weapons and Equipment

In the *Weapons* and *Equipment* sections, various weapons are labeled and described with embedded evaluations of their effectiveness and reliability (see Sections 3.2 and 4.4), which are attitudinal stances of *appreciation*. *Appreciation* relates to "meanings construing our evaluations of 'things', especially things we make" (Martin & White, 2005, p. 56). While the majority of these tokens are negative, especially as they relate to the weapons' *impact* (e.g., *basic*), *quality* (e.g., *heavy*) and *balance* (e.g., *low reliability*), there are also positive tokens relating to the evaluation of the weapons' *complexity* (e.g., *easy to use*) and *valuation* (e.g., *effective*). Balliet's predominantly negative evaluations of the weapons display his awareness of their limitations, anticipating potential *problems* and things that can *go wrong*. As such, the weapon evaluations contribute to *affective* stances of *(dis)satisfaction*.

Balliet's descriptions of weapons highlight his awareness of this tension between the desired functionality (positive *valuation*) and lack of efficacy (negative *balance*). This is perhaps most clear where Balliet uses a typographical strikethrough where the crossing out of words is a way of reflecting the dynamic editing of otherwise static text as in (21):

(21)   Backup gun ~~if~~ when the Luty shits itself.

This functions to express Balliet's negative assessment of the weapons as not a possibility, but a certainty, and indexes his own reflections on the efficiency of the weapon. Such epistemic stances are expressed through *heteroglossic* utterances in which other voices/viewpoints are referenced. The use of the strikethrough displays an awareness of an alternative (the possibility of a weapon malfunctioning) but ultimately *contracts* to close off the reality of this possibility. *Contractive* utterances feature prominently in the *Weapons* section. Although this anticipation for failure would provide a justification for any problems during his attack, the positioning of the weapons as expected to fail sets up a particularly auspicious perception of the weapons should they not fail: That is, the weapons would be seen as beating the odds, and therefore viable. Such stances highlight a main motivating factor for Balliet's attack; despite the sense of anxiety surrounding the weapons' viability, Balliet's objective to use and test them prevails.

The descriptions of the weapons contain highly specific details, including quantified components and measurements as in (22). Such detailed descriptions amplify Balliet's displayed investment in the discourse, thereby strengthening his commitment to the proffered content:

(22)   1x 15 round magazine in the gun, 2x 20 round mags on the right shoulder
         and 15x 15 round mags in pouches on the chest-rig.
         Loaded with 124 grain soft lead bullets and 7 grain chlorate powder (65/35
         potassium chlorate/sugar)

While these may be considered *monoglossic* bare assertions, Gales (2021, p. 683) notes that "assertions [...] may, on the surface, appear to be *monoglossic* but still create tension, due to the backdrop of social context or disalignment with the audience" (also see Gales, 2011 and White, 2015). Indeed, when contextualized as a TVM and viewed in relation to how other far-right extremists have entextualized language and replicated actions of other far-right perpetrators (Kupper et al., 2022; see Section 8.4), these statements serve as references and instructions for others to copy or modify. In this sense, Balliet's statements can be taken up by such anticipated audience(s). Likewise, other audiences that may be disaligned with Balliet (e.g., law enforcement and members of targeted social groups) may be ideologically opposed to his assertations, and these audiences can reflect on these utterances in assessing Balliet's actions. Thus, for the purposes of this study, considering the forensic context, such surface-level *monoglossic* utterances are better understood as *heteroglossic pronouncements*.

The *short pre-action report* also presents images, which, like the detailed descriptions of weapons, enhance the authorial investment. These images demonstrate a realization of the weapons, such that the weapons are presented as physical objects rather than conceptual, idealized items. The incorporation of these semiotic modes (Keane, 2003) in this text makes the weapons "real" by their photographed existence, *provoking* attitude and *texturing* evaluative stances (Martin, 2004).

In the *Achievements* section, as the achievement list unfolds, the targets shift from specified groups of people as in (14) to an unspecified *someone*. This shift corresponds with a shift in focus towards the type of weapons used, as in (23), and a shift in stances, from evaluations of others (*judgment*, discussed in Section 5.2) to evaluations of weapons (*appreciation*):

(23)   Kill someone with the Smith-Carbine.

As Haberl (2020, p. 126) notes, the presence, utilization and glorification of certain weapons can relate to *identity building* efforts with links to ideology, such that references (and uses) of "the weapon itself can indeed become part of a group's narrative and identity." Thus, Balliet's stances towards these weapons function not only as meaning-creations of the weapons themselves but also as a symbolic tool of ideological alignment with the far-right (see also Luckham, 1984; see Sections 4.2, 6.3 and 7.3).

5.2 Evaluations of Targets

In the *Plan* section, Balliet provides evaluations of social groups and the physical spaces associated with (and likely to be occupied by) these groups. While we recognize the social significance and consecrated relationship between these spaces and the social groups, we find that Balliet expresses different stances towards them, warranting an analysis that reflects this distinction.

5.2.1 Evaluations of Social Groups as Targets

As mentioned in Sections 3.2 and 4.2, Balliet identifies his targets in the *Objectives* section: *anti-Whites [. . .] jews preferred*, Balliet's concept of *anti-White* becomes clear throughout the following sections as he refers to various racial, ethnic, religious and political groups. He negatively evaluates them through tokens of negative *affect,* realized as slurs and derogatory reference terms, such as *kikes*, the n-word, and the use of noncapitalized terms (e.g., *jew, muslims*) and tokens of negative *judgment*.

Tokens of *judgment* refer to *judgments* of *social sanction* (ethics: *veracity* and *propriety*) and *social esteem* (behaviors: *normality, capacity, tenacity*). Balliet expresses these *judgments* through metaphorical relations (e.g., *rats* and *golems*), morphological negation (the prefix *anti-*) and semantically encoded lexical items (e.g., labels as in *traitors*). The effect of these negative *judgments* reflects what Etaywe and Zappavigna (2023, p. 6) refer to as *coupling*: "the co-instantiation of an attitudinal expression with an attitudinal target."

These patterned negative *judgments* discursively construct a collective out-group (see Etaywe (2022) on *bond clusters*), creating an *us versus them* dichotomy in which Balliet is positioned in opposition to these groups. Balliet's negative framing is therefore best understood as ideologically driven, and the negative evaluations serve to align him with those who share this evaluative stance. This reflects the *pledges to harm* that Hurt and Grant (2019, p. 159) explore; in focusing on tokens of *judgment*, they note that "a pledge author's concern with the ethical meanings found within *propriety* is, ipso facto, a concern with how just the world is, and thus speaks to the author's possible motivations."

In terms of *Engagement*, the social groups as targets are evaluated in slightly different clausal constructions in different sections. In the *Achievements* section, Balliet *proclaims* who should be killed or how someone should be killed in a series of grammatically similar constructions of the verb *kill* + Object (+ Instrument), as in (23) and (24):

(24) Kill a jew.

In doing so, Balliet *contracts* the dialogic space by "excluding certain dialogic alternatives from any subsequent communicative interaction or at least towards constraining the scope of these alternatives" (Martin & White, 2005, p. 117). Through syntactic repetition, Balliet expresses an *upscaled* authoritative stance insisting how and who should be killed. This contrasts slightly with the clauses in which these targets are discussed elsewhere in the text. For example, (7) uses a similar grammatical structure as (22) and (23), but it contains the modifying language *as many … as possible* and *preferred*. Such mitigating language presents an *expansive* utterance in which alternative perspectives are invited. In this sense, Balliet expresses a *down-scaled* investment in who his targets are, indicating that the means of killing are more important to Balliet than the identity and number of victims.

5.2.2 Evaluations of Physical Spaces as Targets

The physical spaces that Balliet evaluates primarily include a synagogue, but he also mentions previously considered structures including a *mosque* and an *antifa "culture" center.* By choosing and referring to a synagogue as the *target*, Balliet clearly disaligns with followers of Judaism, justifying and legitimizing the target location by noting the potential presence of Jewish people (see Sections 3.2 and 4.2). However, in contrast to the (negative) *judgments* of groups of people framed as targets, the synagogue is evaluated primarily through tokens of *appreciation* (e.g., it being *not a soft target* and having *quite high* security measures), reflecting his perception of its feasibility as a target. While the evaluations of the synagogue are positive tokens of *composition*, for Balliet, they contribute to a negative framing in terms of *reaction*. As such, they are *double coded* (Gales, 2021) to reflect both perspectives from mainstream society and the author's linguistically manifested perspective. Such discursive framing of tensions between positive tokens of *composition* resulting in negative stances of *reaction* reflects far-right beliefs such as the *Great Replacement* conspiracy theory and accelerationism, which require the recognition of stable democracies, (malevolent) coalitions and established governments that are viewed as organized. But it is precisely because the far-right views these institutions and social structures as stable that they become a perceived threat to white supremacy, and are therefore negatively evaluated.

In (25), at the end of the *Plan* section, Balliet reflects on his evaluations of the synagogue target:

(25)   Rereading the paragraph, that really sounds bad. So why, you may ask, did I choose this target.

Despite referring to (his evaluations of) the target (and the plan) as *bad*, the decision is justified by the potential to kill his human targets. This provides insights into Balliet's decision-making process in which the target location is driven by the target population, which in turn is driven by ideological beliefs. Through these expressed stances, it is revealed that regardless of various acknowledged obstacles of the location, his ideology supersedes his rationality. The question posed in (25) is *expansive* in that Balliet anticipates a possible question from readers of the text and thus *entertains* alternative perspectives and signals a disalignment with those of a shared ideology. That is, the question is not posed as rhetorical. Rather, he follows this up by providing a justification for selecting a target, which closes off alternative viewpoints. Even though Balliet continues to describe alternative targets, his expression is understood as *contractive* in that he "invokes a contrary position which is then said not to hold" (Martin & White, 2005, p. 120). In doing so, Balliet invites readers to align with his proposition and justification, assuming that they will subscribe to this "taken-for-granted axiological paradigm" (Martin & White, 2005, p. 121). This reflects a communicative purpose of TVMs, discussed in Section 3.

5.3 Evaluations of Plans

Much of Balliet's discussion of the plan is expressed with *irrealis* markers, realized as desideratives (e.g., Balliet *hopes* the grenades detonate). *Irrealis* markers of (positive) *inclination* provide insights into Balliet's desires (understood here as relating to his motivations). Gales (2021, p. 680) notes that "[c]odings of *irrealis* generally relate to surges of behavior and dispositions of *desire* and *fear*." As Martin and White (2005) note, *irrealis affect* (*inclination*) can be used to look at authorial intention rather than reaction. While expressions of intent do not necessarily equate to psychological intention, we suggest that linguistic manifestations in the context of TVMs, which as discussed previously serve to communicate justifications for violent acts, contain linguistic cues as to the violent intent.

The *Plan* section contains a number of positive *inclination* tokens paired with negative tokens of *appreciation*. This creates a type of push-and-pull dynamic where various behaviors, events and outcomes that Balliet *needs*, *prefers* and will *try* to do are juxtaposed with an awareness of things that could go wrong. This awareness (and expectation) of possible failure is evidenced through multiple tokens of negative *appreciation* of the plan, (e.g., the plan not being *foolproof*, and *sound[ing] bad*). The co-occurrence of *irrealis* markers (positive *inclination*) and negative tokens of *appreciation* relating to the plan contribute to a sense of *affective insecurity* (see Gales (2021) on *implicitly invoked* evaluations).

Evaluations of the plan are mainly presented through dialogically *expansive* clauses. This is done through a series of conditional clauses (e.g., *If . . .*), disjunctive coordinated clauses (e.g., *or, alternatively*), probability modals (e.g., *could*) and hedges and mental-verb projections (e.g., *I think, I believe*). The high frequency of *expansive* clauses relating to Balliet's evaluation of the plan demonstrates low commitment to the specificity of these plans (which does not, however, indicate a low commitment to *act* on these plans, as evidenced through Balliet's actions). Such expansive clauses also contribute to a sense of insecurity.

Negative evaluations of the plan display alignment with the far-right in that his assumed failures are not just a problem for him but for the progress of the far-right in achieving their goals, discussed next.

5.4 Evaluations of Goals

As previously noted, the *short pre-action report* presents a list of goals in the *Objectives* section and a gaming-type list of achievements in the *Achievements* section (see Sections 3.2 and 4.4). These future-oriented objectives and achievements are here referred to collectively as goals in that they present Balliet's expressed intent or purpose. As such, the goals are tokens of *desire* (positive *inclination*) towards which Balliet expresses positive evaluations of *dis/satisfaction* (relating to *the pursuit of goals*, see Martin & White, 2005).

Through his stances towards the desired activities, Balliet positions himself as an active participant in accomplishing the goals; he projects *pleasure* in the desired outcomes of *the Objectives*: *proving* (the viability of improvised weapons), *increasing* (the morale of others), *killing* (specific people) and *not dying*. But, as discussed previously, he also demonstrates frustration through *dissatisfaction* with the weapons, and the things that could go wrong in his plan. These varied stances highlight projected struggles of achieving these goals, which ultimately position them as tokens of positive *valuation* in that they are worthwhile. Not only do the objectives reflect ideological alignments in what Balliet wants to achieve, but the discursive positioning of them as *valuable* amongst evaluations of *dissatisfaction* reflects a strong ideological commitment to these objectives.

The achievements and objectives reveal sometimes competing discourses between his ideologically motivated targets and his ideologically motivated display of weapons. In the *Objectives* section, these are clearly listed as separate goals. But in the *Achievements* section, there is a non-delineated shift in what is being appraised as an achievement. In the achievements with specified targets (see (24)), Balliet is positioned as responsible for the success or failure, questioning his capability (negative *capacity*). However, in the latter achievements that specify the weapons (see (23)), it is the weapons' effectiveness that determines the success of the achievements. These achievements reflect a relationship between intention and action, in which Balliet has personal agency over only some of the goals.

5.5 Evaluations of the Far-Right Community

The preceding analysis has demonstrated how Balliet discursively positions himself as part of the far-right through stances towards weapons and equipment, targets, plans and goals. This alignment is facilitated by a shared set of values, presented as "common sense." Those that share Balliet's expressed ideological perspectives are constructed as the intended reader.

Here, we turn to stances that Balliet takes towards this ideal addressee. Overall, there are few tokens of *attitude* towards his audience, with the exception of the *attitudinally inscribed* epithet *suppressed* (negative *capacity*) in (7), which presents a value position of how he views *other whites*. Moreover, in noting that *moral[e]* needs to be increased, this inscribes an evaluation of negative *tenacity* in that the morale of this group is low. These *judgments* of *social esteem* present an *affective* stance of *displeasure* in how Balliet evaluates this group, framing it as a problem to be solved and effectively providing a justification (and motivation) for his planned violent acts. Notably, such explicit justification is limited to this one statement, suggesting that Balliet assumes ideological alignment with the intended audience in that the justification/motivation is otherwise taken for granted.

As mentioned previously, Balliet's alignment with the far-right is also evidenced through framing himself as part of the in-group of *suppressed Whites*. Moreover, he expresses alignment through pronominal uses of *we* in (26) and direct references to readers as *you* in (25), (27) and (28):

(26)   After all, if every White Man kills just one, <u>we</u> win.

(27)   <u>You</u> know what a knife looks like?

(28)   use 55g and 10g and additional 5ml water if <u>yours</u> is dry and pure.

In (26), the collective group of *every White Man* serves as the antecedent of *we*, positioning Balliet as a member of this group. The positive *valuation* token (*win*) reflects an ideologically driven collective goal, presenting Balliet as one person amongst others working together. In (25), (27) and (28), Balliet addresses an assumed idealized audience (*you*), taking for granted who his readers are. For example, he assumes that the reader knows the answer to his rhetorical question in (27), is similarly preparing weapons (and following his instructions) in (28) and may question his target decisions in (25). His propositions are presented as unproblematic and justified by shared ideological frameworks.

5.6 Evaluations of Stephan Balliet

While the preceding analysis highlights insights into Balliet's presentation of himself (e.g., his feelings, emotions and levels of commitment), the analysis in this section focuses on broader patterns in how Balliet evaluates himself.

One such pattern is the recurring *invoked* connotations of *insecurity*. Negative evaluations (*appreciation*) of weapons, the goals and the plan, together with *desires* of weapon functionality and pursuing objectives, create an implicit stance of *insecurity*. This is also presented through Balliet's negative *judgments* of *capacity* of himself, that is, how (in)capable he views himself. Furthermore, Balliet portrays this insecurity through more overt *inscribed* evaluations through conditional clauses, typographical strikethroughs, hedges, possibility modals and explicit references to failing. These invoked and inscribed stances demonstrate that he presents himself as aware of, and expecting to, fail. Martin and White (2005, p. 49) describe *(in)security* as covering "our feelings of peace and anxiety." As such, Balliet's expressions of *insecurity* are understood as presenting an anxious disposition. This disposition is further discussed in Section 6.3.

As shown in (29), Balliet also provides a physical description of himself through tokens of *normality:*

(29)   as a young, fit, white male with blond hair and blue eyes and without tattoos, piercings or other degenerate shit (beside being a weeb) I already look like a terrorist.

In describing himself as a *weeb*, Balliet evaluates himself with negative *judgment*. He compares his physical appearance with a negatively appraised description of *degenerate shit*, which, from Balliet's perspective, would make his plan more feasible and make him look less like a *terrorist*. This highlights that for Balliet, perceptions of others are important, and that *look[ing] like a terrorist* is an obstacle in acting like a terrorist. In labeling himself as a *terrorist*, he *inscribes* negative *judgment* towards himself.

Balliet also presents positive emotional stances of *happiness*, invoking a sense of humor. This is done through two instances of expressions of laughter (*jej*) and recurring themes of cruel humor (see Sections 3.2 and 4.3).

Another patterned way in which Balliet evaluates himself is through the almost exclusive use of the grammatical first-person singular, save for the one instance in (25). While he may share an ideological agenda with others of the far-right, he presents himself as alone in his actions. Balliet's various expressed stances towards himself contribute to an eventual heroic positioning should he "succeed." Through negative evaluations of his weapons, plans and target location, Balliet positions himself as having to overcome numerous obstacles and expecting to *fail*, so if he does "succeed," he *wins*. This relates to the *quest for significance* discussion in Section 4. This framing occurs amongst the alignment with the far-right, such that despite acting alone, his actions and goals contribute to ideological aims.

5.7 Conclusion

The appraisal analysis provides insight into Balliet's constructed intersubjective positioning and interpersonal meanings with his weapons and equipment, targets, plans, goals, audience and himself. These evaluations reveal a dynamic relationship between his ideological framework and his language use expressed through varied *attitudinal* stances, *contractive* and *expansive* utterances, and *upscaled* and *downscaled* language. Through these discursive means, Balliet presents himself as aligned with the far-right, demonstrating (ideological) motives for his violent actions.

We reiterate that findings of downplayed investment should not be understood as a reduced threat level. For example, the observation that language evaluating the targets and the plan were *downscaled* does not imply that the threat is understood as downscaled. Rather, the findings presented here challenge popular beliefs of threatening language in that such "weak" language is sometimes present in these communications (see Gales, 2010, 2015). This demonstrates that authors such as Balliet rely on a range of linguistic resources to express attitudinal assessments, construct negotiated relationships and identities, and (dis)align with ideological frameworks. As discussed in the following sections, understanding this ideological positioning and how it manifests in language provides insights for our understanding of violent far-right actors and has important implications for improving threat assessment practices and preventing these types of attacks.

6 Retrospective Threat Assessment

6.1 Behavioral Analysis

Lone-actor terrorist incidents generate questions including what in the subject's background and personality characteristics may have motivated that person to attack innocent people.[15] The linguistic data covered in previous sections offers certain clues. This section moves beyond the language evidence created by Stephan Balliet and primarily considers different testimonies from the Halle trial to discuss his life and inform those involved in both researching and investigating lone-actor terrorists about clues that often precede those types of targeted attacks. Some of these violent acts could potentially be thwarted in the future if indicative patterns in the life events, pre-attack behaviors and motives of lone-actor terrorists, along with significant language in their TVMs, can be identified and then reported to authorities (see Section 7).

A logical place to start our behavioral analysis is with an examination of significant life events in Balliet's background, followed by an assessment of his red flags, triggering events and behaviors he displayed as he moved on a pathway towards violence. Court transcripts compiled by Pook et al. (2021) from Balliet's trial were reviewed, translated, summarized, categorized and analyzed for this section. The perpetrator's trial was held in Germany where privacy laws specify that only first names of most witnesses are revealed to the public. For some witnesses who were law enforcement officers, only their job descriptions were publicized without revealing their names. The reader will see testimonial information attributed accordingly. Family members are not compelled to testify in Germany, and none of Balliet's family members did.

---

[15] The main contributors of this section were Sharon Smith and Julia Kupper. In accordance with Dr. Smith's obligations as a former FBI employee pursuant to her FBI employment agreement, this section has undergone a prepublication review for the purpose of identifying prohibited disclosures but has not been reviewed for editorial content or accuracy. The FBI does not endorse or validate any information that Dr. Smith has described in this section. The opinions expressed in this section are hers and not those of the FBI or any other government agency.

6.2 Stephan Balliet's Background

Family Life

Stephan Balliet was born in 1992. His mother, fifty-five years old at the time of his attack, was a primary school teacher, and his father, sixty-two years old, was a mechanic for radio and TV broadcasting networks. Balliet has one half-sister (same mother), Anne, who is about three years older. During his testimony, Balliet reported having good relationships with his family members. After the attack, his mother resigned from her job and attempted suicide. Her suicide note, addressed to Anne, included antisemitic expressions and conspiracy theories, along with her claim that Germany had let her and her son down, thereby destroying him despite her efforts to save him.

Mario, Anne's ex-boyfriend, with whom she has a son, testified that he and Anne ended their romantic relationship when their son was two years old, but both remained involved in their son's care. According to Mario, neither of Balliet's parents had friends. After Balliet's parents' divorce, his mother moved out of the family home. According to Mario, Balliet was reserved and shy when they met. The only time Mario recalled that Balliet smiled was when he played with his nephew.

School

A former colleague of Balliet's mother claimed Balliet was able to verbally express himself well as a preschooler. Although he had no friends, he wanted to be and was the center of attention in his family. His primary school teacher testified that he was a very introverted loner who never allowed any closeness, emotionally or physically, such as being hugged or held. Balliet testified that he was a loner at school without role models or career aspirations. He blamed his small stature and minimal social skills for not being well-liked by classmates. On the stand, Balliet admitted he would have liked to have had a girlfriend, but according to what Balliet shared with a psychologist who assessed him postattack attempts he made to approach girls were unsuccessful.

Military Time

According to Balliet's testimony, his difficulties in establishing friendships continued into his military service. His roommate during basic training testified that Balliet and his other roommates were not compatible. Balliet often complained about physical exercise. Nicknamed the "potato," he was so unathletic that others had to carry his equipment. Balliet received standard training with military weapons but no specialized weapons training. Overall, the roommate described him as a socially awkward person who had difficulty getting along with others.

University Time

After his military service, Balliet enrolled at a university in Magdeburg, Saxony-Anhalt. He began his studies in chemistry in the second semester, doing well with some subjects but not with others. His parents supported him financially, along with a student loan from the government, which caused him to live a modest life.

Illness in 2013

During his university time, Balliet experienced a serious illness in 2013. His testimony did not provide details about this disease, only that he could not move properly for more than one year and still had problems at the time of his trial. A chief inspector from the Bundeskriminalamt (BKA) testified that Balliet's illness, which resulted in a two-week hospital stay and from which he nearly died, could have originated due to misuse of narcotics. During his testimony, Balliet did admit to having taken methamphetamines in the past. Mario testified that he was told Balliet had a potentially life-threatening stomach perforation. Furthermore, the BKA chief inspector testified that after his illness, Balliet did not resume his studies, claiming that he was disappointed in humanity and his doctors. He also did not strive to get better, and eventually stopped making plans for his life. His world diminished to include only his family members. He refused even to go out with his sister who invited him to have beers with her friends, explaining he could not consume alcohol after his illness and did not want to be with others who were drinking.

Social Activities

Mario also described Balliet as sometimes aggressive towards others. Anne and Mario occasionally invited him to parties to get him out of the house after his illness, per the request of his mother who tried different things to get him to socialize. Although he accompanied them a few times, he was standoffish. Jäger and Landes (2020) reported that Balliet made antisemitic and racist remarks in this environment, which were sometimes met with encouragement from the sister's circle of friends. The perpetrator said he never talked about his problems, political leanings or attack plans with anyone.

Employment Status

At some point, Balliet decided he could not work for the German state, as it was *unfair* regarding "wage distribution, working class, all those things." He did not receive unemployment benefits. When Balliet's father pressured him to get a job, Balliet resisted and moved to his mother's residence. His father stopped supporting him financially, so Balliet lived only on 200€ per month, provided by his mother. She also covered his health insurance.

Balliet's Retrospective Viewpoint of his Mass Casualty Event

Balliet's actions led to significant feelings of guilt about how his attack affected his family because he learned that his family members suffered far worse than he imagined due to the press persecuting them. At his trial, the offender testified he also felt guilty about the white victims he shot. However, he showed no remorse about the attack against the Jewish community and his other victims.

6.3 Red Flags, Triggering Events and Pathway Warning Behaviors

Studying various factors such as red flags, triggering events and pathway warning behaviors in perpetrators' lives can help those who analyze these attacks better understand the context in which they are more likely to occur and the psychological factors that are often present when they do occur. However, any single behavior, event or psychological factor is not sufficient to indicate the potential for violent action.

6.3.1 Red Flag Warning Behaviors

Various important events and psychological factors in Balliet's life discussed in what follows are also often present in the lives of other targeted violence offenders, including lone-actor terrorists (Kupper & Meloy, 2023; Kupper, Cotti & Meloy, 2023; Langman, 2009). Clusters of these behaviors can suggest the possibility that someone is at an increased risk for committing violence.

Social Isolation

Balliet grew up in a home where friendships and healthy coping mechanisms were not modeled. When Balliet's mother attempted to commit suicide after his attack, she said neither she nor Balliet had any responsibility for what he did. An introverted loner, the perpetrator testified that he did not have anyone with whom he felt comfortable sharing his political views. After his sickness, he cut off any real-world contact other than with family and online interactions (see all other sections on his strong online ties). His inability to drink alcohol after his illness was his alleged reason for further isolation. Additionally, Dr. Norbert Leygraf, the forensic psychiatrist and neurologist who interviewed Balliet in prison, testified that he displayed tendencies that suggested autism; however, he stressed it is difficult to diagnose autism in adulthood. One of the gaming-style *Achievements* in the *short pre-action report* is headlined *The Way of the Autist*, which may be an indirect way for Balliet to self-identify as autistic. Balliet's social isolation also suggested he lacked purpose until he began his plans and preparation for his attack, which was his *quest for significance* (see Section 4).

Being Bullied/Ridiculed

Balliet testified during his trial that he was bullied in school and in the military. There is a consensus amongst researchers that long-term bullying can play a substantial role in the motivation to conduct targeted school shootings (Cornell & Stohlman, 2020; Musu et al., 2019).

Failure to Find Meaningful Work to Provide Purpose and Financial Success

Balliet's military service was so subpar that he was not sufficiently physically fit to even carry his own equipment. Once he became sick, he was never employed again. When his father cut him off financially, he chose to live with his mother and depend on her for financial support and health insurance.

Externalizing Blame for Dissatisfaction with His Life

Balliet testified that he was unhappy with, even deeply ashamed about, many aspects of his life: physically, relationally and financially. Shame is a painful and powerful emotion resulting from a sense of not being worthy enough to gain the admiration and respect of others (Thompson, 2015). Because shame can cause a psychologically overwhelming sense of unworthiness (see Sections 3.2, 5.3 and 5.6 for evidence of self-doubt and insecurity in his TVM), it is often masked or repudiated by externalizing blame for those inadequacies and failures onto others, which Balliet did in blaming Jewish, Muslim and non-German people for thwarting his career and relationship prospects.

Anecdotal Evidence of Racial/Ethnic Extremist Viewpoints

At a birthday party in 2016, Balliet told Mario that "the fucking Jews are responsible for everything." When asked if he was an *antisemite*, he answered, *yes, I am*. He later added that he also could not tolerate Muslims anymore, as they have been planning to "conquer Europe for the last 1,300 years" (see Sections 3.2, 4.2 and 5.2 on his denigrating views of his target groups in the TVM).

Aggressive Behavior

Balliet once pulled out a knife when arguing with a friend at a birthday party. Another time he aggressively approached two strangers speaking a foreign language and yelled at them for not speaking German.

Failure to Successfully Pair Bond

Balliet's own admissions suggest that he never successfully developed romantic relationships with women.

Radicalization

During his trial, Balliet refused to provide specific information about forums where he was radicalized to "protect the communities." The psychologist who assessed him stated Balliet's deeply radicalized beliefs were so entrenched that they were almost impossible to change (see all other sections on his strong affiliation with far-right communities).

Weapons Skill and Excessive Interest in Weapons

Balliet's military experience provided him with basic weapons training. According to the prosecutor's closing arguments, his preexisting extreme fascination with guns prompted him to start building his own firearms for the attack (see Sections 3.2, 4.4, 5.1 and 7.3).

Lack of Conscience and Empathy

As a white male German, Balliet viewed Jewish, Muslim, black and non-German people with contempt, an emotion that relegates others to a subhuman or nonhuman status. He was frustrated that he failed to kill any Jewish victims during his attack. Balliet's prison psychologist testified that he noted a pattern of detachment and emotional coldness in his interpersonal relationships. This lack of conscience and empathy is also reflected in his TVM (see Section 3.2).

Sense of Entitlement and Superiority

Balliet thought it regrettable that his mother and sister did not have more children or stay at home as housewives. He chose not to support himself or even apply for social benefits but instead relied on his family for financial support.

Diagnosis of Personality Disorders

Dr. Leygraf, the forensic psychiatrist who assessed Balliet, painted a picture of a clumsy, inhibited loner with unstable self-esteem (see Sections 3.2, 5.3 and 5.6

for signs of insecurity in his TVM). He also determined that Balliet had a basic paranoid mistrust, thinking he was constantly controlled and spied on, which prevented him from building trusting relationships. He opined Balliet's abnormalities corresponded to complex personality disorders, specifically schizoid and paranoid. Balliet showed significant deficits in emotional responsiveness, describing his victims as *collateral damage*. After his illness, in some ways Balliet almost became like a child again, living in his room at his mother's place and being taken care of by her physically and financially. His personality disorders and life situation made him more prone to absorbing and manifesting ideological thoughts and conspiracy theories because these allowed him external explanations for his situation and poor prospects. His lack of emotional affectability to the suffering of others enabled him to draw up a meticulous plan of action with the aim of killing as many people as possible, motivated by his desire for recognition and attention (see Sections 4.4, 5.6 and 8.1).

Behavior Suggesting Some Psychopathy Traits

Although Balliet's psychiatric diagnosis did not mention psychopathy, his lifestyle suggested he displayed some traits discussed that are consistent with that disorder, specifically lack of empathy and conscience (see Section 3.2), sense of entitlement, parasitic lifestyle, externalizing blame and lack of realistic, long-term goals (Smith et al., 2012).

6.3.2 Triggering Events

Lone-actor terrorism attacks are complex events; however, they are often preceded by triggering events in the perpetrators' lives. During Balliet's trial, various witnesses offered explanations of events in his life that they believed may have triggered his attack.

Illness in 2013

After Balliet's illness, he spent years becoming radicalized online while constructing homemade weapons and ammunition (see Sections 4.3, 5.1 and 7.3). He apparently gained some degree of social acceptance by sharing his knowledge of weapons and ammunition construction with other dark web participants. One witness at Balliet's trial opined that his lack of money provided an important motivation for his attack, that is, he was able to demonstrate that he could do *something* with little money and homemade weapons (see Sections 3.2, 4.4, 5.1 and 7.3 on his prioritization of his weapons).

Refugee Crisis in 2015

According to a BKA chief inspector's testimony, the *refugee crisis* in 2015 was a turning point for Balliet, as the influx of refugees motivated him to spend three years building eight weapons. The 3D printer Balliet used was in his room in his father's house but thinking the printer was only a toy, his father never saw the perpetrator building his weapons, nor was he even aware of their existence. The constructed firearms and explosives were stored in Balliet's locked rooms in his father's and mother's homes (see Section 7.3).

Brenton Tarrant's Attack in 2019

Balliet testified that Brenton Tarrant, who killed fifty-one and injured forty during a mass shooting at two mosques in New Zealand in March 2019, became his role model (see Sections 7.3 and 8.3). Balliet was inspired that a white man *fought back*. Similarly, Balliet "wanted to speak out against the replacement of Germans." The first time he became aware of the *Great Replacement* conspiracy (see Sections 4.2, 5.2 and 7.2) was in reading Tarrant's TVM, but this viewpoint fit with his perception of what had been happening in Germany since 2015.

6.3.3 Pathway to Targeted Violence Analysis

An important question law enforcement considers after violent events is: Were there warning signs leading to the violent action that, if detected, might have enabled someone to intercede to prevent the violence? (see Section 7). Security authorities' goal of preventing violence is often achieved by intervention of bystanders, or due to their reporting concerns to authorities about the subject's behavioral clues. In this section, we examine what we learned from trial testimony about the significant behaviors in which Balliet engaged as he moved along a pathway towards violence to determine if any of those behaviors were obvious enough that his attack could have been prevented.

Calhoun and Weston's (2023, 2003) pathway to intended violence includes six stages, starting with a grievance before engaging in research, planning, preparation or implementation behaviors of breaching and attacking.

Feeling a Grievance

While the *Great Replacement* conspiracy narrative may have fueled Balliet's grievance, his isolation and lack of friends and girlfriends, along with bullying in school and the military, may have provided a foundation for his alienation from society. He chose to live-stream his attack to prove that it could be committed with homemade weapons to motivate imitators all over the world, likely with the goal of becoming a *saint* to online far-right movements (see also Sections 4.3, 7.2 and 8.4). Some of those around him believed his expressed hatred of others was, in part, his way of explaining away his personal, financial, career and relationship failures.

Ideation

Subjects with grievances have options for resolving their injuries or injustices. Balliet likely believed successfully executing his attack against his target group would resolve his issues and finally give meaning to his existence (see Section 4).

Research/Planning

After Balliet's illness, he spent his time researching how to construct weapons, explosives and ammunition and studying previous attackers (see Sections 7.3). During his trial, several witnesses testified that his violent act was partly inspired and triggered by Tarrant, whose modus operandi Balliet apparently studied meticulously to enhance the operational success of his own attack. Furthermore, Balliet justified shooting one of his lifeless victims repeatedly after she was on the ground because Philip Manshaus' attack on August 10, 2019 at a mosque in Norway had failed when a worshiper, whom he had shot, held onto his foot, thus preventing him from carrying out his mass casualty event. This highlights the phenomenon that lone actors often commit similar terrorist attacks because they share means, motivations and opportunities and learn tactical necessities from previous attackers (see Section 8.1).

Preparation

Actors take steps to research how to commit their intended attack and then plan and prepare its successful implementation. In an act exemplifying predatory behavior, Balliet deliberately chose Yom Kippur, the holiest day in the Jewish calendar, because more Jewish people would be in a synagogue (see Section 7.3). His plan was to kill men, women and children. He originally wanted to attack a mosque, perhaps to emulate his *idol*, Tarrant (see Sections 4.2, 5.2, 7.3 and 8.3). To incorporate both ideas, after leaving the synagogue, he intended to attack an Islamic culture center.

One week after Tarrant's terrorist attack, Balliet began jogging, intensified constructing weapons and started producing ammunition. He began working on his *legacy tokens* (R. F. Tunkel, personal communication, September 25, 2023) on March 26, 2019, starting with his TVM nine days after Tarrant's attack. He created his *READ THIS FIRST* document next and then the file

"Manifesto," completing it three days before his attack. He bought a phone with a high-quality camera for live-streaming in the spring of 2019, and purchased wireless loudspeakers on October 1, 2019. Balliet first gained information about the targeted synagogue's location and entrances via satellite images online; then in late summer 2019, he took surveillance trips in his mother's car. He also studied the layout of the adjacent cemetery and court-yard from the outside. Additionally, he tested his live-stream capability for the attack and rented a car to drive to the synagogue on October 7, 2019. The following day and one day prior to the attack, Balliet loaded his weapons and ammunition into the car, prepared his explosives and withdrew the remaining 600€ from his account, likely to use for an escape.

Breach

Balliet's plans for breaching were not sufficient, since he was unable to get inside due to the synagogue's heavily secured doors.

Attack

On the morning of his crime, Balliet uploaded his written documents, casually said goodbye to his mother, stored his remaining weapons in a bag and left. Unable to breach the synagogue, he shot a woman walking by and then shot at, but missed, a bystander who rushed to her aid. After leaving the synagogue and on his way to the Islamic culture center, he spontaneously chose a kebab shop because, in his mind, it was related to the Muslim culture. He also attempted to run over a black man while fleeing from the police.

6.3.4 Could the Halle Terrorism Attack Have Been Prevented?

Stephan Balliet's act of violence killed two innocent people and terrorized not only his targets in Halle but also exemplified the security risk of lone-actor attacks (see Section 7). However, prevention can occur if family, friends or acquaintances detect the perpetrator's warning indicators and report them to law enforcement or other appropriate authorities in time.

The question in this case is: How much of a threat did Balliet's family and acquaintances perceive him to be? Could Balliet's psychological red flags and behaviors, as he moved along a pathway towards violence, have been detected, thus enabling someone to prevent his deadly terrorist attack? Although signs of Balliet's psychologically fragile ego, his political views and grievances were known to his family members, they were not perceived as warning signs and thus not reported to security authorities (see Section 7.3)..

6.4 Conclusion

Balliet's life was marked by failures in several significant areas. Socially awkward, he was bullied and humiliated in school and the military. Unable to maintain mentally challenging and financially stabilizing work, he also failed to establish romantic relationships with women and even friendships with anyone outside his family. Lacking healthy coping mechanisms, Balliet turned his anger and frustration outward away from his own failures. Instead, he projected blame onto non-Germans and refugees who began immigrating into Germany *en masse* in 2015. He also blamed Jewish people whom he considered the masterminds of the *Great Replacement* conspiracy against white men. It appears he may have tried to alleviate his internal pain with illicit drugs, leading to his life-threatening illness that probably only increased his resentment and isolation. Balliet's alienation, paranoia, entitlement, irresponsibility, lack of empathy and need to blame others likely fueled his racism and radicalization, which led him down the pathway to violence. Tarrant's attack in 2019 became the catalyst he needed to energize him into action. Constructing his weapons, explosives and ammunition finally gave his life purpose and illuminated, in his mind, a goal worthy of elevating him to the status of a revered figure in the terrorist community. Like Tarrant, Balliet wanted to be admired as someone who could construct death dealing tools and carry out an attack against their jointly perceived enemy, a plan that likely offered some relief from his wounded self-image. Balliet arrogantly boasted of his xenophobic views and the knowledge he acquired on the dark web to the prison psychiatrist, yet underneath he likely was an ashamed, unhappy victim, full of rage, blaming others for the inadequacies in his life. Insecure and displaying abnormalities corresponding to schizoid and paranoid personality disorders, according to the psychiatrist, along with some characteristics associated with psychopathy, he lacked resilience and had woefully inadequate coping skills.

As discussed in the next section, better understanding the dangerousness posed by lone-actor terrorists can assist security authorities in investigating their crimes and potentially intervening in some cases to prevent violence.

7 Lone-Actor Investigative Challenges

7.1 Security Constraints

The attack on the synagogue in Halle is one of a worldwide series of targeted violence events committed by lone-actor terrorists that security authorities and experts from various disciplines have classified as far-right terrorism

(Europol, 2020; Thorleifsson & Düker, 2021).[16] In at least six attempted or completed mass attacks that occurred between October 2018 and October 2019 in Pittsburgh (US), Christchurch (NZ), Poway (US), El Paso (US), Bærum (NO) and Halle (DE), far-right motives were identified as the main ideology. This is substantiated by (1) the choice of targets (Jewish, Muslim and black communities), (2) comparable patterns in the planning and execution of their crimes (Manemann, 2020; Schattka, 2020; Wahlström, 2020), and (3) the self-reports published by the perpetrators, namely TVMs (Kupper & Meloy, 2021; see Sections 3, 4, 5 and 8).

From a security and statistical perspective, the likelihood of being targeted in a mass attack is minimal as terrorism events are infrequent and have a low base rate (Bundeskriminalamt, 2023; Europol, 2023). However, the impact and fear of such incidents remain profound, causing widespread concerns – especially for often-targeted populations – due to their unpredictable nature, severe consequences and societal effects. Some of the potential offenders may display concerning behaviors or commit other crimes prior to their attacks; however, the challenge for security measures lies in detecting individuals who radicalize (online) in near-isolation, and who often plan covertly over extended periods, leaving limited intervention opportunities (see Sections 4.2, 5.2 and 6.3). The central question here is whether assessing the particular dangerousness of these individuals from the available information is possible pre-attack, or if such information justifies intervention by investigative or intelligence agencies.

Subsequent to the Halle event, the actions of security authorities, primarily law enforcement, became the subject of public scrutiny and debate. This prompted a domestic political discourse and resulted in the establishment of the *19th Parliamentary Committee of Inquiry* within the state parliament of Saxony-Anhalt, Germany. The Committee's investigation focused on evaluating the assessment of the threat situation pre-attack, the effectiveness of implemented security measures and the execution of police operations on the day of the incident (Striegel, 2021). Moreover, Balliet's trial delved into various aspects of his pre-event behaviors, including an exploration of his personality (see Sections 6.2 and 6.3), the police's investigations of his online and offline preparatory indicators and the authorities' broader understanding of *lone-actor terrorists* (Pook et al., 2021).

The following examination encompasses (1) security authorities' findings of the threat Balliet posed pre-attack, (2) retrospectively gathered insights into his personality and (3) preparatory digital and on-the-ground behaviors he demonstrated in the lead-up to the event. Notably, Balliet's radicalization only became

---

[16] The main contributors of this section were Marcus Papadopulos and Julia Kupper.

apparent through meticulous retrospective analysis, collating information gleaned from court proceedings and subsequent criminal investigations following his act of targeted violence. The report of the 19th Parliamentary Investigation Committee of the state parliament of Saxony-Anhalt (Striegel, 2021) and the documentation of the trial against Balliet (Pook et al., 2021) served as the basis for this section, along with data from academic studies and publications on the phenomenon of far-right lone-actor terrorism (e.g., Dittrich et al., 2022; Ellis et al., 2016; Manemann, 2020; Thorleifsson & Düker, 2021). This review is neither an evaluation of the police work in the run-up to, or on the day of, the attack but intended to assess the information on which the security authorities were able to base their pre-incident actions, and the extent to which the Halle perpetrator showed potential warning signs prior to the attack.

7.2 Challenges in Detecting Lone-Actor Terrorists

Preventing lone-actor attacks is dependent on the early identification of subjects of concern who are a potential threat to national security. At the same time, recognizing indicators of radicalization that precede a serious, targeted violence act is one of the greatest challenges for intelligence and investigative authorities. Particularly when warning indications appear sporadically in various places or are only indirectly recognizable, security agencies often reach the limits of their abilities to detect potential risks at an early stage (see Section 6.2).

Particularly in far-right online ecosystems, shared ideological narratives are visible on various platforms where these types of perpetrators tend to radicalize as hatred is incited and serious acts of violence are advocated (see Prologue and Sections 4.3, 5.5 and 8.4). The communities' reliance on anonymous access, encrypted communication and platform operators' minimal content control and reluctance to cooperate with authorities are all key factors in facilitating online radicalization (Gerster et al., 2021; Guhl, Ebner & Rau, 2020; Pook et al., 2021). Perpetrators of the most severe attacks and with the *highest kill counts*, such as Anders Breivik and Brenton Tarrant, are glorified as *saints* in virtual forums, reinforcing enemy stereotypes and eliciting allegiance to them (Manemann, 2020; see Sections 4.3, 6.3 and 8.4). The recurring connecting themes in these digital spaces include the idea of an all-controlling "Jewish world conspiracy," for example, the *Great Replacement* (see Sections 4.2, 5.2 and 6.3). In particular, toxic ideals of masculinity, along with a desire for a patriarchal, hierarchically organized world under the dominance of white men, play an important identity-forming role for this subculture (Thorleifsson & Düker, 2021).

Thus, security agencies need to consider the crucial role of digital spaces and online warning behaviors in combination with on-the-ground activities when potential perpetrators mobilize to violence (Kupper & Meloy, 2023). Once alarming offline behaviors – such as interactions with extremist groups – prompt reports to authorities, it is vital to examine the individual's online activities, including social media profiles. A structured approach that explores openly accessible digital spaces with ideological inclinations serves as a starting point for preventive actions (e.g., investigations or ongoing monitoring) to avert potential threats (Amman & Meloy, 2021; Papadopulos, 2022). At this juncture, security authorities grapple with the vast communication avenues used by far-right actors on online platforms, which in itself creates challenges in gathering and evaluating terrorism-related information. Identifying users within digital spaces is complex due to concealment tools and platform privacy policies. Additionally, targeted data acquisition or surveillance by law enforcement demand indications of concrete plans for acts of targeted violence in Germany. Although intelligence agencies have a lower threshold for this type of monitoring, transmitting data on an impending event to the police would occur at a relatively late stage. Hence, preventative law enforcement actions heavily rely on information from bystanders, domestic authorities or foreign intelligence and call for extensive investigative efforts.

7.3 The Halle Terrorism Case

Alongside other attackers in 2018–2019 and beyond, Balliet belonged to a group of lone-actor terrorists who radicalized in far-right digital spaces, both on the clearnet and darknet (Kupper et al., 2022). This section discusses challenges faced by security authorities when dealing with such offenders, including an examination of Balliet's behaviors in the run-up to his crime. This is particularly relevant for organizational considerations that involve preventative law enforcement measures, as these are crucial in identifying at what point in time and to what extent information on these types of solo protagonists is available to security authorities pre-attack.

7.3.1 Pre-Halle Evaluations of Germany's Threat Landscape

Threat assessments form the basis for the implementation of police protection concepts as well as preventative measures against potential targeted violence offenders. When assessing threats in connection with ideologically motivated crimes, the process is grounded in a standardized scheme. Based on national and international – investigative and intelligence – information, the German Federal Criminal Police Office (BKA) prepares basic analyses in the form of situational reports on politically motivated crimes and makes these available to the State Criminal Police Offices (Landeskriminalämter or LKAs). Germany has had a heightened threat level related to far-right terrorism for many years, and in June 2018 the BKA published a general threat assessment on far-right motivated crimes (Striegel, 2021). However, security authorities had no concrete indications of immediate or imminent threats to persons, objects, institutions or events in the lead-up to the Halle incident. The BKA's situational report indicated a general threat to Jewish institutions, in particular from the far-right extremist scene, but there was no intelligence about specific circumstances or persons of concern that were known to the authorities at this point in time.

After the attacks in Pittsburgh (October 2018) and Christchurch (March 2019), communications between the BKA and LKAs did not result in any changes to the overall threat level of lone-actor terrorism events (Striegel, 2021). According to the BKA's assessment, such attack scenarios were still considered unlikely for Germany, even though several mass shootings targeting synagogues and mosques occurred between 2018 and 2019. The investigation by the *Specialist Investigation Unit 5* of the Halle police station and the LKA of Saxony-Anhalt (that is, the local and regional police authorities) into media reports on the attacks in Pittsburgh and Christchurch had not revealed any indications that would have led to an adjustment of the threat situation for their areas of responsibilities. There were therefore no indications that would have fundamentally intensified the assessment of a "not specified" threat situation for Saxony-Anhalt (Striegel, 2021).

Moreover, the situational report disseminated by the BKA to the federal states was supplemented by the LKAs with their own specific analyses and subsequent guidelines, which were then forwarded to the regional and local law enforcement agencies. The local police forces expanded their risk analyses with regional considerations and used them as a basis for drawing up their own protection concepts on how to take measures against potential threats (Striegel, 2021).

Nonetheless, no specific threats to Jewish institutions on Yom Kippur were identified by the regional or local police forces in Saxony-Anhalt in 2019 or in previous years. Before the Halle incident, there were also no indications of a change in the threat level by police in this region, and no specific security inquiries or reports of conspicuous behaviors that would have indicated serious criminal offenses against the Jewish community. A representative of the community in Halle did report that he had been receiving antisemitic letters for years, which had been forwarded to the police for investigation. However, there were no risk indicators that would have led to a tightening of the security situation at synagogues in the Halle area. The crime landscape against Jewish institutions and antisemitic incidents recorded by the police in Halle, such as damage to property, had not changed this either. It should be noted that Balliet was never connected to any of these crimes in and around Halle, neither according to the results of the 19th PCI nor the court proceedings (Striegel, 2021).

For the police's assessment of the threat situation, especially in Halle, there was thus no concrete indication of an imminent attack from the far-right extremist spectrum, and no explicit analyses at regional and local police stations pointed towards a replication of targeted violence acts that had occurred abroad. The scenario of a lone-actor terrorism attack in Germany was also described as unlikely by the BKA (Striegel, 2021).

7.3.2 Balliet's Personality and Pre-Attack Behaviors Through an Organizational Lens

Early identification of individuals on the pathway to violence relies on observable warning signs, both online and on-the-ground (Calhoun & Weston, 2023, 2021, 2003; Kupper & Meloy, 2023). Behaviors that might indicate a progression towards violence or radicalization are most often noticeable within a person's social environment, such as behaviors at home, school or work. The following segment employs an organizational perspective for security authorities to review Balliet's personality, online and offline conduct and his journey towards violence, using the court trial transcripts (Pook et al., 2021).

One expert witness, Dr. Lisa John, a psychologist, revealed the following assessment that was conducted during Balliet's detention: the perpetrator was described as having an IQ of 105 and average intelligence, and the psychological tests carried out on him indicated a complex personality profile. He appeared to be inhibited, dissatisfied with himself and the world, pessimistic, reserved, self-deprecating and socially awkward (see Sections 3–5 on how many of these traits are evident in his TVM). In addition, she reported that he had difficulties coping with everyday life, had psychosomatic complaints, a pronounced adherence to moral principles and the belief that he was superior to others. Balliet emphasized that many of his current problems were due to bad luck, that is, external circum-stances (see Sections 6.2 and 6.3). According to the psychologist, he may have concealed his unpleasant character traits or problems but expressed that if given the opportunity, he would repeat his violent actions (Pook et al., 2021). Although Balliet's life reflected personal difficulties and problematic personality traits, from an organizational-legal standpoint, none of these would have suggested a high risk of committing a mass casualty attack. Thus, they would not have met the threshold for early detection and intervention by the police.

Forensic psychiatrist Professor Dr. Leygraf opined on the issue of Balliet's criminal responsibility for the Halle aggression (see Section 6.3). In his expert opinion, Balliet did not want to give the impression that he was mentally ill or that his attack was connected to personal grievances because those excuses would, in Balliet's view, deprive his attack of what he perceived as ideological heroism. Leygraf testified that Balliet had culpability: "Even if the act was justified from the defendant's point of view, he was very aware that the act was fundamentally contrary to society's values" (Pook et al., 2021, p. 569; see also Section 5.6 on Balliet labeling himself a *terrorist*). Additionally, in Leygraf's opinion, it was therefore "overwhelmingly likely that the accused would commit similarly serious crimes again if he had the opportunity" (Pook et al., 2021, p. 571).

7.3.3 Relevant Offline Behaviors

This section retrospectively examines Balliet's problematic offline behaviors that security authorities could have potentially detected prior to his attack, specifically delinquency, identity and worldview, violence or legitimization of violence, affinity for and access to weapons and planning and preparation of the attack (Guldimann & Meloy, 2020; von Berg, 2019).

Delinquency

Balliet had not come to the attention of the security authorities before his attack. He had no previous convictions, nor had he appeared as a potential far-right terrorist in any database. Because he feared being monitored by the Federal Office for the Protection of the Constitution, Germany's domestic intelligence agency, he never joined an organized far-right extremist group and had no known contacts in the far-right (offline) scene.

Identity and Worldview

Some statements that Balliet made in his family environment were characterized as xenophobic, antisemitic and anti-Muslim (see Section 6). He was convinced of an all-controlling "Jewish world conspiracy" and the *Great Replacement*, and his enemies were derived from these conspiracy narratives. He was aware that those around him did not fully share his ideological views, and thus only communicated them cautiously in order to avoid discussions about his beliefs with others. According to the court records, there were reports from Balliet's extended (offline) social circle about his anti-Jewish and xenophobic views (Pook et al., 2021). However, these do not appear to have crossed the *limits of what can be said* societally – and in some cases were even common practice in his environment of acquaintances (Jäger & Landes, 2020). Therefore, these behaviors did not lead to reports to the security authorities.

Violence or the Legitimization of Violence

Balliet legitimized the use of violence to defend his existence and that of the white race, which became his *quest for significance* (see Section 4.1). He was also prepared to accept the killing of innocent people as collateral damage and to die with honor in a battle against his enemies. During his trial, his sister's ex-boyfriend mentioned that Balliet pulled out a knife at a party during an argument (see Section 6.3). However, this was not reported and therefore did not result in any criminal charges, which could have put him on security authorities' radar.

Passion for Weapons

Balliet exhibited a heightened interest in weaponry from an early age, notably escalating after purchasing a percussion rifle (muzzleloader) in 2015 and subsequently advancing to crafting his own firearms via a 3D printer (see Sections 3.2, 4.4, 5.1 and 6.3 on his extreme weapons fascination). His focus on constructing his own guns intensified in 2016, influenced by his perceived concerns about immigration. He accessed weapon designs and improvised explosive device manuals through various online platforms, for instance on the darknet. Following the Christchurch attack, Balliet altered his mindset: transitioning from a self-defense victim orientation to crafting weapons for the explicit purpose of committing crimes as a warrior, aligning his methods with the approach adopted by Brenton Tarrant (see Sections 6.3 and 8.3). However, none of these behaviors were reported to the authorities.

Planning and Preparation of the Attack

During the planning phase, Balliet maintained extreme secrecy about both his ideology and intentions. He deliberately refrained from sharing his political views and concealed his plan to commit an act of targeted violence – even from his family – the only offline social circle with whom he sustainability engaged in (see Section 6.3). His meticulous planning involved selecting a location and date, surveilling his primary target and studying previous attackers' TVMs and live-streams. The reconnaissance of his primary target began in the summer of 2019 and included exploring the grounds of the synagogue using his mother's car and studying the layout of the cemetery. Furthermore, he chose the date for his attack, Yom Kippur, so that he could have killed as many people as possible. Balliet also focused on the online dissemination of his crime, conducting tests to ensure smooth live-streaming from the synagogue by checking mobile phone reception in the area. He acquired equipment, including a combat helmet, a ballistic vest, a sword, knives and firearms he had been constructing since 2015/2016. Moreover, over three years, he produced eight weapons and amassed 1,364 rounds of ammunition, some engraved with swastikas and "SS" runes. Balliet tested his firearms discreetly in his father's shed and utilized a homemade silencer, actions that seemingly did not raise suspicion in the vicinity despite their potential external impact. As mentioned previously, when initiating his crime, Balliet followed the pattern of other attackers in 2018–2019 by publishing a TVM and live-streaming the incident. He had painstakingly prepared these elements in advance, mirroring the methods of his predecessors (see Section 8.3).

7.3.4 Relevant Online Behaviors

Balliet carefully avoided disclosing information that could have exposed his online associates to scrutiny by security authorities, limiting investigators to data available on his computers and storage devices only. Consequently, their examination of his online contacts yielded inconclusive findings (Pook et al., 2021). Following his illness in 2013, Balliet withdrew from society, immersing himself in virtual spaces like imageboards and online games after relocating to his mother's apartment (see Section 6.3). Balliet increasingly identified with this diffused community that conceptualized itself as representatives of the "white race." During this period, Balliet encountered far-right extremist content on various platforms, reinforcing and solidifying his xenophobic, antisemitic beliefs and conspiracy narratives that likely had roots in earlier stages of his life (Jäger & Landes, 2020). These ideologies were shared and amplified within the online environment with which he engaged, deepening his involvement with far-right ideology and glorifying previous violent acts committed by figures celebrated in that subculture (see Section 8.4). His collection of materials included snuff videos and music from groups such as the *Hamas-Brigades* (in reference to a Palestinian terrorist group), the *Wehrmacht* and the *Waffen SS* (both expressions from Nazi Germany). Moreover, Balliet prepared the media presentation of his planned attack on the internet.

7.4 Consolidated Assessment

As detailed in Section 7.3, the 2018 BKA situational report highlighted a general terrorism threat level from Germany's far-right extremist spectrum but lacked details on specific threat scenarios (Striegel, 2021). The Pittsburgh (2018) and Christchurch (2019) mass casualty events did not heighten concerns about domestic terrorism in Germany and security authorities deemed such attack scenarios unlikely. Additionally, there were no indications of imminent threats in Saxony-Anhalt or specific security inquiries from the Jewish community regarding Yom Kippur in 2019.

The retrospective assessment of the Halle threat situation raises questions about whether Balliet exhibited any overt security-related behaviors before the attack that could have flagged him as a threat to authorities, both online and offline. However, to identify Balliet as a potentially radicalized perpetrator would have required some form of evidence, which security authorities lacked. Indeed, witnesses testified during his trial that Balliet was socially withdrawn with latent insecurities. His tendency to isolate himself and lack of interaction made it difficult for others to recognize and interpret potential warning signs before the attack.

Balliet's conduct epitomizes a dangerous blend of far-right extremist ideologies, a validation of violence on his *quest for significance* and an intense preoccupation with weapons; however, these relevant behaviors were not reported to security authorities. Furthermore, his intentions for planned violence through a terrorism attack were not publicly disclosed until minutes prior to the event, aligning with a common strategy of operational secrecy to maximize the attacker's success. Even an earlier reported threat involving Balliet using a knife was either concealed or tacitly accepted within his social circle. He managed to hide his weapon design and construction, even from his family, utilizing a 3D printer stored in his father's house, though parts of the assembled weapons were housed in his parents' home. The percussion rifle he obtained in 2015 did not trigger security authority intervention as it could be legally purchased without a permit from the age of eighteen and was thus not registered in Germany's National Weapons Register. Consequently, it was not documented to be in Balliet's possession; however, even if the weapon had been registered, he likely would not have been detected due to his covert preparatory actions. Although Balliet's family did not express any concerns about his firearm possession, their stance could not be further explored during the trial as they declined to testify.

Balliet managed to keep his offline activities, including his weapon construction, hidden from detection. However, combining his online engagement in far-right extremist circles, interest in past attackers, equipment procurement and focus on potential targets could have raised alarms for security authorities if he had already been flagged as a concern by authorities, such as Germany's domestic intelligence agency. Individually, and acknowledging our hindsight bias when drawing these conclusions, these factors might not have triggered assessments, but identification within a politically motivated group could have prompted surveillance measures, for instance. Regardless, Balliet did not fit this profile and had not drawn attention as a potential threat, and pre-incident detection was almost impossible in this case. Despite the analyses in Sections 3, 4 and 5, which identified Balliet's alignment with the far-right, his TVM was not available to security authorities pre-attack, as it was only disseminated minutes prior to him driving to his target location, thus providing no time for intervention.

7.5 Conclusion

Stephan Balliet represents a lone-actor terrorist who submerged into an expansive global far-right online community as an anonymous user where he underwent unnoticed radicalization within a very limited offline social circle until carrying out an act of targeted violence. The Halle case demonstrates the legal and factual limitations of preventative measurements if concerning behaviors are not recognized and reported to security authorities that can assess the level of risk an individual might pose. Despite the challenges encountered by security authorities, there are potential strategies to address the threat of lone-actor terrorists. Studying the behaviors, actions and communications – and particularly the movement from online to on-the-ground preparatory activities – in a structured approach helps identify potential traits and patterns. In addition, improved information sharing between investigative and intelligence services aids in early threat detection and mitigation.

The next section evaluates the impact of preceding lone-actor attacks on the Halle shooter and the uptake of Balliet's attack and communications in different online ecosystems of the far-right.

8 Contagion and Copycat Uptakes

8.1 The Contagion and Copycat Effect

Within the world of terrorism and threat assessment, intertextual links and references between targeted violence perpetrators' communications have been tied to contagion and copycat effects, as evidenced in the writings of offenders that committed ten seemingly unrelated transnational far-right terrorist attacks, including the Halle incident (Kupper et al., 2022).[17] *Contagion* alludes to the imitation of the violent act in an acute period – usually several weeks – following a publicized mass casualty incident (Kupper et al., 2022). *Copycat* refers to a chronic phenomenon – generally extended over months or years – and involves the imitation of both the act and actor (Kupper et al., 2022; van der Meer, Meloy & Hoffmann, 2017). Kupper et al. (2022) corroborated the emergence of a new, complex genre set of different interrelated text

---

[17] The main contributors of this section were Julia Kupper and Marie Bojsen-Møller.

types that has become increasingly consolidated in form and function, consisting of TVMs and live-streams, attack announcements on online platforms and writings on equipment utilized during the attacks. The strategic goal of inciting others to violent action with do-it-yourself guides for lone-actor attacks is part of the authors' terror orchestration, intended to circulate ideological motivations, operational strategies and tactical advice in furtherance of inspiring the next imitator (Kupper et al., 2022; Kupper, 2022). The presence of shared lexical and structural components across these types of language evidence indicates the traceable links between the consumption of violence-justifying content and self-radicalization in the online sphere (Kupper, Rękawek & Kriner, 2023). This intertextuality between perpetrators signals that they study previous TVMs and live-streams and use them as templates during the planning and preparation, mobilization and implementation phases (Kupper et al., 2022). In other words, the _illicit genre set_ of TVMs and live-streams is _taken up_ by subsequent far-right terrorists (Bojsen-Møller et al., 2020; Kupper et al., 2022). In the following section, we outline the framework of _uptake_ (Freadman, 2002), which forms the basis of our analysis of the intertextual links and the immediate and later uptakes – reactions and responses – that followed the Halle attack.

8.2 Uptake as Intertextuality

Genres are intertextually connected to other genres or to manifestations of the same genre. This means that genres influence each other in a multitude of ways, for instance by indirectly referencing or even directly quoting earlier utterances. These interconnections are called _uptakes_ (Freadman, 2002; see also Bojsen-Møller, 2021). Uptakes are defined as all explicit reactions and responses that a given genre receives. As such, they are "part of the perlocutionary domain" of utterances (Bojsen-Møller, 2021, p. 101), which has to do with "the feelings, thoughts, or actions of the audience" (Austin, 1962, p. 101). The term uptake was originally coined by Austin (1962), but we use Freadman's (2002) understanding of uptake, which is primarily inspired by Bakhtin's (1986) concept of _dialogism_ (see Section 3.1 on _addressivity_). Dialogism refers to the fact that all utterances are inherently dialogic, which means that they will likely receive responses and reactions from others. Such uptakes can consist of responses from the audience, for instance in the form of expressions of outrage towards an utterance, direct intertextual references or links to preceding utterances belonging to the same genre.

Uptakes can roughly be divided into _immediate_ and _later_ categories, which may vary considerably (Bojsen-Møller, 2023) as demonstrated in the following.

Since the genre of TVMs is intrinsically linked to the author of the documents and, if realized, to the act of targeted violence that follows it, our analysis will not only focus on uptakes of Balliet's communications but also on uptakes of his attack and references to his name. In accordance with this, Freadman (2020) argues that the *agent* (the author) of a genre, the genre itself and the social action that the genre is tied to, all coincide. This claim is substantiated by the fact that intertextual links and references between perpetrators can be tied to contagion and copycat effects (Kupper et al., 2022).

In order to assess a possible contagion and copycat effect across and beyond Stephan Balliet's attack, we conducted a manual, qualitative content analysis of the offender's written and spoken language evidence and examined the transcripts from his court trial (Pook et al., 2021). This was completed to analyze any potential intertextual links, that is, uptakes, to other targeted violence communications connected to acts of violence that preceded this incident. For the second part of the analysis, we investigated four sets of data: (1) different types of targeted violence communications from terrorism incidents that succeeded the Halle shooting; (2) archived threads from several imageboard forums that were obtained from extremism research colleagues; (3) over 200 channels on Telegram; and (4) numerous testimonies from the Halle trial. This was conducted to analyze how Balliet's communications and his attack were taken up by others in different online settings.

8.3 Uptakes by Stephan Balliet

The contagion and copycat framework laid out in Kupper et al. (2022) suggests that perpetrators often:

- reference names of notorious same-genre authors in their TVMs or on the weapons they display during live-streams;
- copy structural components and cite, rephrase or plagiarize textual elements from previous writings or recordings; and/or
- include self-interviews in a Q&A format in their communications that mirror self-interviews made by other targeted violence offenders.

In comparison to preceding and succeeding lone-actors that committed attacks motivated by far-right sentiments, Balliet's publicized written and spoken language evidence does not entail any direct references to names of infamous predecessors or explicit citations from previous texts. However, his unpublished self-interview titled *Your F&A Guide* – the German equivalent of *Q&A guide* – includes an explicit example of the copycat effect and was inspired by previous self-interviews in terms of layout and structure.

Brenton Tarrant's attack in New Zealand was one of the triggering events that mobilized Balliet to violent action (see Sections 6.3 and 7.3). It is perhaps unsurprising that the only clear reference to a previous attacker across all of Balliet's materials is a direct mention of Tarrant in his self-interview in (30):

(30) *Is there anyone you want to thank?*
      Yes, Brenton Tarrant.
      Before his glorious Operation, I was nearly completely black-pilled about
      the future. Around the great brown flood in 2015 I first started to gear
      up.[18] [...] But seeing that Mad Cunt lighting up dozens of ragheads like
      an ancient avatar of war lit up something inside me I thought was long
      gone, maybe even never really there in the first place. I can only
      describe it as the faint echo of our racial soul. Yeah, maybe whites have
      already lost, maybe there is no hope. *So what?* If we are destined to
      vanish, why not go out fighting?

In this quote, he directly explicates how Tarrant's attack and ideological stance have been primary sources of inspiration for his own act of violence. This copycat effect is also reflected in the structure of the self-interview, which includes intertextual links to earlier instances of the genre: In terms of structural components, the entire *Your F&A Guide* consists of twenty-three questions, two of them being identical to Tarrant's Q&A in his TVM: *Who are you?* and *Are you a Racist?* (Kupper et al., 2022). Balliet's self-interview is thus both structurally and ideologically an uptake of previous examples of the genre of Q&As written by targeted violence offenders.

8.4 Uptakes of Stephan Balliet's Communications and Attack

8.4.1 Immediate Uptakes on "the Chans" and Telegram

Karolin Schwarz, a German researcher and expert on online far-right extremism, testified during the Halle shooting court trial that she began monitoring direct uptakes of Balliet's attack, TVM and live-stream on different imageboards in the immediate aftermath of the incident (Pook et al., 2021). Schwarz gave evidence that the first reaction to the attack itself occurred at 01:07 PM (approximately one hour after the start of the act of violence) on Kohlchan, a German derivation of the imageboard 8chan. Users on this platform were the first to reference the initial press release circulated in the mainstream media (Pook et al., 2021). Several other posts followed on the imageboards 4chan and Meguca, as well as Telegram, an instant messaging service that is commonly utilized by (far-right) extremist groups (Kupper & Dittrich, 2024; Pook et al., 2021). Meguca was the platform where Balliet announced his attack at 11:57 AM

---

[18] Refugee influx in 2015–2016.

in the *Meadhall* thread, publishing his TVM and distributing a link to his live-stream. Three minutes after the post, the first Meguca user commented with "deadpost and a twitch link awfully suspicious but I'm a dumb [n-word], so I'll bite" (Meguca, 2019). This was followed by several users screenshotting and commenting on Balliet's self-made weapons and ongoing live-stream, such as "Looks solid, I like the schizo-type posting in the readme txts" and "HE'S FUCKING EVERYTHING UP AAAAAAAAAAAAAAAAAA This is fucking clumsy" (Meguca, 2019). The discourse in this thread continued until 10:22 PM on the day of the attack when users decided to "bin [delete] everything" (Meguca, 2019). These uptakes thus ranged from praising the posts made by Balliet to ridiculing his failures during the attack.

On Kohlchan, the first uptakes of Balliet's targeted violence live-stream were identified between 05:00 and 06:00 PM in the form of numerous posts in the sub-board /pol/,[19] which also resulted in subsequent comments on Telegram (Pook et al., 2021). Users on Kohlchan discussed how to save and spread the live-stream, and exchanged views on the weapons used by Balliet during the attack, joking about them malfunctioning (Pook et al., 2021). These forms of intertextual links provide evidence of the close reading of Balliet's documents and watching of the live-stream by his targeted audience. Quickly thereafter, memes were created, ridiculing the perpetrator, his failed mission and low kill count, for instance by spreading a meme titled *Virgin German vs. Brenton T.*, which was spread on 4chan (Pook et al., 2021, p. 591–592). This also highlights the immediate comparison between perpetrators in these types of online spaces.

Some imageboard users also speculated about the motivations for the Halle synagogue shooting, suggesting that the event might have been fueled by the following motivations: race/ethnicity, jihadism, involuntarily celibate, anti-government/-authority (particularly the Reichsbürger movement) and mental illness (Pook et al., 2021). The German Reichsbürger movement refers to a diverse assortment of individuals and small groups, the "Citizens of the Empire" that deny the legitimacy and authority of the contemporary German state order and its institutions (see, for instance, Kupper & Dittrich, 2023). "Involuntarily celibate," or short "incel," refers to an online subculture of heterosexual men who blame society and women for their lack of romantic success. Others proposed that the attack could have been a "false flag" operation, which refers to a deliberate act committed with the intent of disguising the actual source of responsibility and blaming another party; discussions like this often arise on imageboards after mass casualty events.

---

[19] /pol/ is an abbreviation for "politically incorrect" and refers to a subforum on imageboards.

Yet other comments were found on the imageboard Meguca where users were actively encouraged to share recordings of the online broadcast of his act of violence; other discourse included the police and press (Pook et al., 2021). Further discussions on Kohlchan were concerned with whether or not Balliet was part of the imageboard communities because of a particular sentence he used in his live-stream: "100% Fail haben wir selten hier," which translates to "we hardly ever have a 100% fail here," commenting on the failure to successfully implement an attack against his targets (Pook et al., 2021, p. 591). Users deliberated that this type of language is commonly utilized on Kohlchan and deduced that he must be "one of theirs," according to Schwarz (Pook et al., 2021, p. 591). On Neinchan, an imageboard that was accessible on the darknet, users spread numerous memes mocking the Halle shooter. This included images with the question *Who would win?* with the options of *Holocaust denier* along with a picture of Balliet's face, or *Wooden door*, with an image of the synagogue's entrance.

8.4.2 Later Uptakes

Uptakes by Subsequent Lone-Actor Terrorists

The legacy of the communications and actions associated with attacks such as Balliet's are in a tradition of those aspiring to achieve the admired status of *saints* within the militant accelerationist movement, which celebrates successful lone-actors in far-right online ecosystems such as Terrorgram and "the chans" (Kriner & Ihler, 2022; Kupper, Rękawek & Kriner, 2023). Terrorgram "is a loosely connected network of Telegram channels and accounts that adhere to and promote militant accelerationism" (Kriner & Ihler, 2022), blending the words *Telegram* and *terrorism*.[20] Militant accelerationism is "a set of tactics and strategies designed to put pressure on and exacerbate latent social divisions, often through violence, thus hastening societal collapse" (Kriner, 2022), a belief that is often utilized by the far-right to advance solo terrorist actions. As Macklin (2022, p. 224) has explained, the "dark fandom" of *saints* or martyrs within this online far-right ecosystem (see Sections 4.3, 6.3 and 7.2) is comparable to the heroization of school shooters and serial killers. It therefore moves beyond the copycat aspect and evolves into a *cultural script* for others to follow (Kupper et al., 2022). After the New Zealand mosque shootings, the perpetrator Brenton Tarrant was immediately valorized within the far-right online milieu and started being compared to medieval saints in memes and other forms of online images (Macklin, 2022).

---

[20] See Kriner et al. (2024) and Dittrich et al. (2022) for more information on Terrorgram's evolution.

Since the act of violence in Halle in October 2019, we identified two lone-actor terrorists that directly referenced Balliet in their targeted violence communications, which again shows that both the physical acts of violence and the textual products of terrorism offenders are imitated and taken up by subsequent copycats. The most clear-cut example of Balliet's influence and impact on successive attackers is the case of Hugo Jackson, who, motivated by far-right sentiments, stabbed one of his teachers with nonfatal injuries at his school in Eslöv, Sweden (Kupper et al., 2022). During his interrogation, Jackson stated that he was inspired by Brenton Tarrant, Stephan Balliet and Anton Lundin Pettersson[21] (Lunds Tingsrätt, 2021). Several direct, intertextual uptakes of Balliet's live-stream, as well as references to his name, were evidenced in Jackson's targeted violence communications (Kupper et al., 2022):

- A quote from Balliet's live-stream was written on Jackson's bedroom wall: "Hi my name is Anon, and I think the holocaust never happened. Feminism is the cause of decline of the West which acts as a scapegoat for mass immigration and the root of all these problems is the Jew" (Lunds Tingsrätt, 2021, p. 159).
- Copying his *idol* Balliet, Jackson live-streamed his attack on Twitch and also uttered the words "Ah, Scheiße" (the German equivalent of "oh, shit") twice, a direct reference to Balliet's broadcast, who used identical words when his equipment malfunctioned (Lunds Tingsrätt, 2021, p. 473).
- Balliet's name was written on the skull mask worn by Jackson during the incident (Lunds Tingsrätt, 2021, p. 183).

The quote on the bedroom wall creates an intertextual link to the ideological stances of Balliet, that is, that he has a strong antipathy towards feminism, mass integration and Jewish people – all themes of the *Great Replacement* conspiracy theory (see Sections 4.2, 5.2, 6.3 and 7.2). The fact that whole sections ("Hi my name is Anon [. . .]") and even specific German phrases ("Ah, Scheiße") that Balliet used are repeated by Jackson shows how linguistic imitation and imitation of acts of extremist violence often go hand in hand. The reference to the Halle shooter's name on Jackson's skull mask is likely a way of paying homage to Balliet as a hero and to treat him as one of the *saints* of the far-right extremist community.

The second perpetrator that referenced the Halle assailant multiple times is Payton Gendron, who conducted a mass shooting at a supermarket in Buffalo, New York, in May 2022 (Kupper & Meloy, 2023). Gendron makes three references

---

[21] Anton Lundin Pettersson perpetrated a targeted stabbing attack at a school in Trollhättan, Sweden in October 2015 (Erlandsson & Meloy, 2018).

to Balliet in his online diary, which he disseminated on Discord – a messaging platform popular amongst gamers – approximately thirty minutes prior to his attack. These references are not uptakes of the *language* of Balliet but, rather, uptakes on his *act of violence* and *references to his name* (see (31) and (32)):

(31) Jimboboiii – 03/11/2022 [. . .] Mistakes will be made. Stephen Balliet and John Earnest are examples. [. . .] What's important is to honor these men who at least tried, and to learn from their mistakes so future attackers don't repeat them. Stephen's mistake was that he had improvised weaponry that didn't work and couldn't make it in the synagogue.

(32) Jimboboiii – 03/11/2022 [discussing which names to write on his firearms that would be used during the act of violence] I had Stephen [Balliet] and John [Earnest] removed from this list because they were unsuccessful, but I'm keeping them in because they had the balls to fight back

While Gendron thus primarily focuses on the fact that Balliet's weapons did not work properly during the attack, he does also praise his bravery and chooses to glorify his actions by writing Balliet's name on his weapon of choice. This kind of uptake, referencing the author of a text, can be seen as a metonymic way of referencing the person's actions and communications, which is then part of the same uptake chain.[22]

In addition, there is a direct uptake of one of Balliet's communications in Gendron's TVM, namely a reference to the Halle shooter's live-stream (see (33)):

(33) **Tools**
    GoPro Hero7 Black:
    This is the tool that would live stream the attack on Twitch. I chose Twitch because:
    1. It was compatible with live streaming for free and all people with the internet could watch and record.
    2. A previous attack was recorded on Twitch (Halle Synagogue Shooting) that lasted about 35 minutes, which for me shows that there is enough time to capture everything important.

In (33), the importance of being able to "capture everything important" is mentioned as the primary goal in Gendron's uptake of Balliet's live-stream. This confirms Kupper et al.'s (2022) conclusion that live-streams are crucial instruments of propaganda for far-right terrorists.

Lastly, it has been argued by Kupper et al. (2022) that Gendron modeled his *Goals* section after Balliet's *Objectives* segment, and also copied other structural components from his TVM, such as adding pictures of his firearms that

---

[22] We thank Dr. Sune Auken for enlightening discussions on this.

would be deployed during the shooting, along with the headline *The Weapon* and a description of the gun, in his writings. It can be anticipated that all of these documents will inspire and incite further acts of violence within the far-right sphere. The uptakes by Hugo Jackson and Payton Gendron verify that both the modus operandi and the communications of previous attackers are studied by subsequent terrorists for a successful implementation of an impending event. However, while Gendron only mentions Balliet's name and live-stream, Jackson quotes his TVM and live-stream directly.

Uptakes on Terrorgram

Balliet's name and references to his attack, TVM and live-stream continue to be circulated within far-right online ecosystems. Schwarz testified that users on Telegram were also quick to circulate content on the Halle attack in the immediate aftermath of the shooting (Pook et al., 2021). Several screenshots of Balliet's live-stream and direct quotes from the perpetrator's broadcast were initially disseminated to glorify the act of violence and express support for his efforts. However, Schwarz later noted a shift to labeling the assailant a "loser," rejecting him because he killed two Germans (Pook et al., 2021, p. 591 and 593). Lone-actor terrorists with less successful attacks than perpetrators such as Robert Bowers, Brenton Tarrant and Patrick Crusius are often "mercilessly mocked and lampooned" in the form of memes that highlight pitfalls (Macklin, 2022, p. 226). However, some of them are still declared *saints* by the Terrorgram community, likely to keep the momentum going and support even failed attackers to continuously incite others to violence (A. Ritzmann, private communication, December 2023). Although Balliet failed to claim instant *saint* status, it was awarded to him at a later stage by the Terrorgram community, despite his low kill count but because of his high efforts to encourage further acts of lone-actor terrorism.

A corpus of 318 Terrorgram channels and 1,864,007 messages that were composed between March 23, 2017 and June 6, 2024 was analyzed for this study by CEMAS (Center for Monitoring, Analysis and Strategy), a nonprofit organization that examines right-wing extremism, disinformation and conspiracy theories. A concordance search for "Stephan Balliet" revealed that references to the Halle shooter intermittently surfaced in posts since October 2019 (see Figure 2).[23] The highest number of mentions in 2021, 2022 and 2023 occurred in the month the attack was carried out, October, likely as a form of remembrance. Balliet has also been officially included in several "Days of Action" *saint calendars*, which highlight specific dates relevant to the names

---

[23] We thank Miro Dittrich for this assessment.

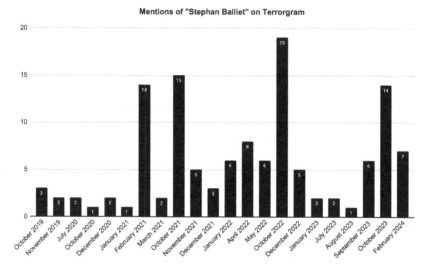

Figure 2 Terrorgram posts related to Stephan Balliet.

of lone-actor terrorists associated with the militant accelerationism movement, providing details of their respective attacks, for example, date and kill count. Further mentions on Terrorgram included news articles about Balliet's trial and attempted escapes from prison. Other channels linked him to articles related to Mr. Bond, a neo-Nazi musician, who was arrested in 2021, because Balliet played one of his songs during his live-stream. In other posts, the perpetrator was labeled "Saint Brenton Tarrant's 4th Disciple," which designates him as one of the assailants that succeeded Tarrant's attack and who made a reference to him. These uptakes directly signal a belonging to this community and highlight a strong copycat and contagion effect of these events.

Additionally, Balliet was lionized in Terrorgram's *White Terror* production, a twenty-four-minute video that was released on the Telegram channel *White Terror* on October 14, 2022. The documentary celebrates 106 individuals for their attacks on a diverse range of targets that occurred from April 1968 to May 2022; some of these perpetrators are depicted as having achieved *sainthood* within the Terrorgram community (Accelerationism Research Consortium, 2022). Particular praise is attributed to perpetrators who live-streamed their attacks, which will likely encourage future broadcasts of targeted violence acts (Kupper & Dittrich, 2024). Theoretically, the difference here between what we could call "uptake as saint" and "uptake as loser" of Balliet shows the complex and unpredictable nature of uptakes; an author can never fully anticipate the reactions that may follow their utterance.

8.5 Conclusion

In this section, we have evidenced a variety of responses and reactions that occurred in (1) Balliet's targeted violence communications, (2) several online far-right ecosystems, including "the chans" and Terrorgram, and (3) different genre sets of subsequent lone-actor terrorists associated with the militant accelerationism movement.

Balliet only made one direct reference to a preceding attacker (Brenton Tarrant) in an unpublished Q&A-style document. However, his attack and targeted violence communications had an indisputable influence on two subsequent lone-actor terrorists (Hugo Jackson and Payton Gendron) during their radicalization, mobilization and implementation phases, as can be seen through their uptakes of his name, TVM and live-stream.

Moreover, Balliet's act and communications were heavily taken up by digital communities in comparable sequences: First reactions and responses focused on the Halle attack itself in the form of written comments on imageboards and messenger apps. Later, this evolved into the dissemination of Balliet's TVM and live-stream, which either occurred in distributing the original materials, or spreading them in the form of direct quotes, screenshots, memes and other visual formats, thus creating complex intertextual chains. We note that such later uptakes had different evaluations of Balliet's attack, which were expressed with distinct terms and memes. These two contrasting themes formed a discourse battle between praising and ridiculing the perpetrator and the event. All of these examples not only illustrate an interlaced network of uptakes across different text types but also a strong contagion and copycat effect in the community of *saint*-pursuing emulators with the goal of inciting violence in the form of a mass casualty events.

9 Discussion

9.1 Forensic Linguistic and Threat Mitigation Takeaways

Stephan Balliet carried out his attempted mass casualty event solitarily and, in this sense, he can be classified as a lone-actor terrorist.[24] Nonetheless, the common thread linking the findings of our analyses is his yearning to be part of *something* larger: the intricate, online far-right ecosystem where assailants with a *high kill score* are lionized as *saints*. His language delineates the communities that he aligns with and orients towards, with his separate communications deliberately constructed to form intertextual links – both internally within the genre set and externally to a plethora of discourse contexts and online

---

[24] The main contributors of this section were Julia Kupper and Marie Bojsen-Møller.

subcultures that he makes relevant in his writings. In all its complexity, Balliet's TVM functions as a Rorschach test of co-alignment with his intended audience: Those who recognize and respond to the pattern of overlayed objectives and in-group references will be able to take up the mantle from him and continue on the quest to counter the *Great Replacement* through acts of violence.

The genre analysis accentuated the communicative functions of Balliet's TVM by examining the genre labels he used, which shed light on the motivations behind his writings and – thus indirectly – behind his attack. The analysis detailed how he tailored his document towards his desired audience by choosing to prioritize his self-made weapons and operational plans with insider knowledge and darkly humorous elements to engage with his readers. The genre section also yielded important takeaways for threat assessment professionals: A self-deprecating, humorous tone and lack of details regarding planning an attack in the communications of a possible future violent terrorist should not be taken as an indication of low probability of a realized attack.

The text linguistic section revealed that Balliet's TVM signaled in-group membership in a network of partly overlapping communities: adherents of far-right conspiracies, weapons constructors and the "extremely online." In add-ition, his objectives were assessed to be strategic rather than tactical, that is, providing a template for other extremists to construct their own weapons, and thus encouraging further attacks. The text linguistic analysis also provided the significant result that weapons and violence fascination can trump specific targets or extremist ideologies for far-right terrorists. It also underlined how internet citizenship and affiliation with online gaming communities play an important role in lone-actor terrorism cases, which confirms findings in the genre section regarding the importance of connecting to an in-group.

The appraisal analysis provided insight into how Balliet's expressed stances demonstrated his ideological framework, his alignment with the far-right and his insecurities regarding his own abilities and chances of success. Through the expressed stances, it became evident that his belief system overpowered his rationality, for instance when selecting his primary target location, the syna-gogue. Additionally, the stance section offered the important insight for threat assessment professionals that a subject's expression of insecurity regarding their own abilities or beliefs in the viability of their plan for a targeted violence act is not an indication of reduced threat level. This corroborates earlier research that finds mitigating language to be present in realized threats and pledges to harm (Gales, 2010, 2015; Hurt 2020).

The retrospective threat assessment emphasized that Balliet was a loner that did not have any real-world friends and only communicated with close family members, despite his interactions with various online communities. It also showed that it was not until Brenton Tarrant conducted his mass shooting in March 2019 that Balliet felt elevated to conduct his own targeted attack against their jointly perceived enemies. Moreover, the behavioral analysis yielded critical information on some of the red flags and warning indicators that family and friends might recognize and act upon before a targeted violence attack, that is, Balliet's far-right sentiments, social isolation and previous violent incidents. The information on his issues of self-esteem is in line with the findings of self-deprecating and insecure language use in the genre, text linguistic and stance sections, and his lack of empathy is also evidenced in the genre section.

The organizational review highlighted that Balliet was not on the radar of any intelligence or investigative agencies in Germany as he was able to shield his online and offline preparatory activities from the external world. This was mainly due to his overall low visibility and secrecy in planning the attack, since no concerning behaviors had been recognized or rather reported to authorities. Balliet was not recognized as being part of an extremist movement, had no criminal history and did not test his weapons outside of his family environment. Hence, he was not singled out as a subject of concern by security agencies and remained below a threshold for preventative law enforcement measures. This corroborates the findings of the threat assessment section that the public is the *first line of defense* in the fight against mass casualty events.

The uptake analysis considered how actual readers and intended audiences responded and reacted to Balliet's attack and utterances by creating intertextual links to his TVM and live-stream in different online ecosystems, such as "the chans" and Terrorgram. Furthermore, it was corroborated how subsequent far-right terrorists have taken up the Halle shooting in their targeted violence communications that were associated with attempted and executed mass casualty events. Lastly, the uptake assessment showcased the vital significance of the interconnectedness and intertextuality between violent attackers, thereby further evidencing the circle of contagion and copycat effects on multiple levels (Kupper et al., 2022). The analysis confirms findings from the genre, text linguistic and stance sections regarding the importance of in-group connections in the Halle terrorism case.

9.2 Concluding Remarks

Looking backwards in the form of a retrospective analysis allows us to move forward in our aims of detecting and preventing future acts of targeted violence. Overall, the results depict a scene of a secluded male who methodologically moved along the pathway to violence in secret and silence, meticulously preparing for his act over several months. In his *quest for significance* and in the fight to "save" the white race against the conspiratorial *Great Replacement*, Balliet followed in the footsteps of preceding attackers while simultaneously paving the way for succeeding copycats. In addition to aligning himself with his in-group of extreme right online subcultures, the Halle shooter disaligned with his targeted out-groups, particularly non-whites "threatening" the existence of his ethnic group. This ideological framework is reflected both throughout his targeted violence communications and modus operandi of the attack when he selected preplanned and spontaneous targets. Having a diverse range of targets not restricted to any specific location, but rather reflective of where out-group populations frequent, allows transnational violent actors to deem and evaluate local target locations as appropriate. Within the far-right belief system, different victim groups can be selected to counter the alleged *Great Replacement*, such as the Jewish, Muslim and black communities, which all became targets during the Halle attack. Even though his plan to kill Jewish and Muslim people failed, Balliet's rampage resulted in killing other random victims. Seeking an end to his misery, Balliet created even more suffering – for his family, the families and friends of those he attacked and any future victims of those who may choose to copy his behavior. This highlights the critical importance of studying lone-actor terrorists, like Balliet, and sharing knowledge gained about their behaviors and writings, in the hope of preventing future attacks.

Signs of personal grievances and extreme ideologies that might evolve into a desire to conduct a targeted attack might be intercepted by bystanders becoming *upstanders* in advance (Federal Bureau of Investigation, 2015). Families, friends, coworkers, classmates and other non-law enforcement observers tend to be the first to detect concerning behaviors when an individual moves along the pathway of intended violence and can act as an early warning system if the threat reporting is destigmatized. Thus, it is imperative to continuously educate the general population about risk factors and warning behaviors, for instance in the form of workplace violence workshops or instructional events at educational facilities. The careful observation and reporting of such indicators are essential to assist intelligence and investigating authorities in assessing the level of threat of an impending attack, formulating mitigation strategies and therefore preventing these types of terrorism attacks. This is accentuated by the fact that most perpetrators disseminate their TVMs or links to live-streams in the minutes or hours prior to an attack, which tends to result in no time for intervention.

9.3 Limitations and Future Research

All data are retrospective and thus subject to the authors' hindsight and confirmation biases. We have attempted to mediate this concern with careful assessments and discussions and numerous systematic, internal peer-reviews of each section by all six authors. To enhance the reliability and validity of the study, we focused on primary sources created by Balliet for the forensic linguistic analyses; however, the threat assessment and organizational review relied on secondary sources, which introduces perceptual biases. Lastly, the confidential nature of the *Your F&A Guide* file limits the replicability of the analysis.

The data and findings of this Element provide a wealth of ideas for future studies. For instance, we originally intended to analyze Balliet's targeted violence live-stream, particularly the bilingual code-switching between English and German. However, we decided to predominantly focus on the written language evidence in this Element and will publish our findings from the analysis of the spoken corroboration in a separate study. Furthermore, we intended to explore the inherent tension between the dynamic interplay of security and freedom of speech when working in a threat assessment context to mitigate future acts of targeted violence. This becomes particularly relevant when examining the intervention thresholds for preventive police measures within the legal framework "freedom, security and justice" from the European Union. These assessments will also be published as separate projects.

References

Accelerationism Research Consortium. (2022). *Intelligence Bulletin: White Terror*. November 2022.

Allchorn, W., Dafnos, A. & Gentile, F. (2022). The role of violent conspiratorial narratives in violent and non-violent extreme right manifestos online. *Global Network on Extremism & Technology*, March 22. https://gnet-research.org/wp content/uploads/2022/03/GNET-Report-The-Role-of-Violent-Conspiratorial-Narratives.pdf.

Amman, M. & Meloy, J. R. (2021). Stochastic terrorism: A linguistic and psychological analysis. *Perspectives on Terrorism*, 15(5), 2–13, Issue Online: https://www.jstor.org/stable/27073433.

Auken, S. (2021). Genres inside genres. A short theory of embedded genre. *Discourse and Writing/Rédactologie*, 31, 163–78. https://doi.org/10.31468/dwr.883.

Austin, J. L. (1962). *How To Do Things with Words*. London: Oxford University Press.

Baele, S. J. (2019). Conspiratorial narratives in violent political actors' language. *Journal of Language and Social Psychology*, 38(5/6), 706–34. https://doi.org/10.1177/0261927X19868494.

Bakhtin, M. M. (1986). The problem of speech genres. In C. Emerson and M. Holquist, eds., V. W. McGee, trans., *Speech Genres and Other Late Essays*. Austin: University of Texas Press, pp. 60–102.

Bartlett, J. & Miller, C. (2010). *The Power of Unreason: Conspiracy Theories, Extremism and Counter-Terrorism*. London: Demos.

Bauer, K., Grunwald, D. & Sicker, D. (2009). The challenges of stopping illegal peer-to-peer file sharing. *NCTA Technical Papers*. Washington, DC: NCTA – The Internet & Television Association.

Bauman, R. & Briggs, C. L. (1990). Poetics and performances as critical perspectives on language and social life. *Annual review of Anthropology*, 19(1), 59–88. https://doi.org/10.1146/annurev.an.19.100190.000423.

Bedingfield, W. (2021). How the far right exploded on Steam and Discord. *Wired*, August 12. www.wired.com/story/far-right-took-over-steam-discord/.

Berger, J. M. (2018). *Extremism*. Cambridge, MA: The MIT Press.

Bergmann, E. (2018). Kinds of conspiracy theories. In E. Bergmann, ed., *Conspiracy & Populism*. Cham: Palgrave Macmillan, pp. 19–45. https://doi.org/10.1007/978-3-319-90359-0_2.

Biber, D., Johansson, S., Leech, G., Conrad, S. & Finegan, E. (1999). *Longman Grammar of Spoken and Written English*. Harlow: Longman.

Bjørgo, T. & Ravndal, J. A. (2019). Extreme-right violence and terrorism: Concepts, patterns, and responses. *ICCT Policy Brief*. Hague: The International Centre for Counterterrorism.

Bojsen-Møller, M. (2021). *The Illicit Genre of Threatening Communications. A Combined Rhetorical Genre Studies and Forensic Linguistic Analysis of Danish Threatening Communications*. [Doctoral dissertation, University of Copenhagen, Denmark]. https://static-curis.ku.dk/portal/files/308491099/Marie_Bojsen_M_ller_The_illicit_genre_of_threatening_communications.pdf.

Bojsen-Møller, M. (2022). Fit to provoke fear? Uptakes and textual travels of threatening communications in legal genres. *International Journal of Speech, Language and the Law*, 29(1), 1–36. https://doi.org/10.1558/ijsll.18869.

Bojsen-Møller, M. (2023). Joke or threat? Competing genre uptakes in a Danish court case. *Language and Law / Linguagem E Direito*, 10(1). Pre-print.

Bojsen-Møller, M., Auken, S., Devitt, A. J. & Christensen, T. K. (2020). Illicit genres: The case of threatening communications. *Sakprosa*, 12(1), 1–53. https://doi.org/10.5617/sakprosa.7416.

Booth, A. (2023). Fractured in-group identity (re)negotiation in an online white nationalist forum. *Applied Corpus Linguistics*, 3(3), 1–8. https://doi.org/10.1016/j.acorp.2023.100062.

Bracke, S. & Hernández Aguilar, L. M. (2023). The politics of replacement: From "race suicide" to the "great replacement." In S. Bracke, L. Manuel and H. Aguilar, eds., *The Politics of Replacement: Demographic Fears, Conspiracy Theories, and Race Wars*. London: Routledge, pp. 1–19.

Bucholtz, M. & Hall, K. (2005). Language and identity. In A. Duranti, ed., *A Companion to Linguistic Anthropology*. Malden: Blackwell, pp. 369–94.

Bundeskriminalamt. (2019). Beschuldigtenvernehmung [interrogation of accused].

Bundeskriminalamt. (2023). *Polizeiliche Kriminalstatistik 2022*. T01 Grundtabelle - Fälle. www.bka.de/SharedDocs/Downloads/DE/Publikationen/Polizeiliche Kriminalstatistik/2022/Bund/Faelle/BU-F-01-T01-Faelle_xls.xlsx?__blob=publicationFile&v=3

Bundesamt für Verfassungsschutz. (2022). *Verfassungsschutzbericht 2021*. www.bmi.bund.de/SharedDocs/downloads/DE/publikationen/themen/sicher heit/vsb-2021-gesamt.pdf?__blob=publicationFile&v=6

Calhoun, F. S. & Weston, S. W. (2003). *Contemporary Threat Management*. San Diego: Specialized Training Services.

Calhoun, F. S. & Weston, S. W. (2021). Rethinking the path to intended violence. In J. R. Meloy and J. H. Hoffman, eds., *International Handbook of Threat Assessment*, 2nd ed., New York: Oxford University Press, pp. 392–406.

Calhoun, F. S. & Weston, S. W. (2023). Imagining the unimaginable to prepare for the unthinkable: Criteria for detecting, reporting, and acting to thwart intended violence. *Journal of Threat Assessment and Management*, 10(3), 188–201. https://doi.org/10.1037/tam0000200.

Cornell, D. G., Gregory, A. & Fan, X. (2011). Reductions in long-term suspensions following adoption of the Virginia student threat assessment guidelines. *NASSP Bulletin*, *95*(3), 175–94. https://doi.org/10.1177/0192636511415255.

Cornell, D., Sheras, P., Gregory, A. & Fan, X. (2009). A retrospective study of school safety conditions in high schools using the Virginia threat assessment guidelines versus alternative approaches. *School Psychology Quarterly*, 24(2), 119–29. https://doi.org/10.1037/a0016182.

Crawford, B. & Keen, F. (2020). The Hanau terrorist attack: How race hate and conspiracy theories are fueling global far-right violence. *Combating Terrorism Center Sentinel*, 13(3), 1–8. https://ctc.westpoint.edu/hanau-terror ist-attack-race-hate-conspiracy-theories-fueling-global-far-right-violence/.

De Beaugrande, R. A. & Dressler, W. U. (1981). *Introduction to Text Linguistics*. London: Longman.

Dietz, P. E. (1986). Mass, serial, and sensational homicides. *Bulletin of the New York Academy of Medicine*, 62, 477–91.

Dittrich, M., Rathje, J., Manemann T. & Müller, F. (2022). *Militant Accelerationism: Origins and Developments in Germany*. Berlin: Center für Monitoring, Analyse und Strategie. https://cemas.io/en/publications/militantaccelerationism/ CeMAS_Militant_Accelerationism_Origins_and_Developments_in_Germany .pdf.

ECRI: European Commission against Racism and Intolerance (2016). *ECRI General Policy Recommendation No. 15 on Combating Hate Speech*. Strasbourg: The Council of Europe.

Ellis, C., Pantucci, R., van Zuijdewijn, J. et al. (2016). *Lone-Actor Terrorism, Final Report: Countering Lone-Actor Terrorism Series*. London: R.U. Studies. https://static.rusi.org/201604_clat_final_report.pdf.

Erlandsson, A. & Meloy, J. R. (2018). The Swedish school attack in Trollhättan. *Journal of Forensic Science*, 63(6), 1917–27. https://pubmed.ncbi.nlm.nih .gov/29684937/.

Etaywe, A. (2022). *Language as Evidence: A Discourse Semantic and Corpus Linguistic Approach to Examining Written Terrorist Threatening Communi cation*. [Doctoral dissertation, University of New South Wales]. http://hdl .handle.net/1959.4/100727.

Etaywe, A. & Zappavigna, M. (2023). The role of social affiliation in incitement: A social semiotic approach to far-right terrorists' incitement to violence. *Language in Society*, 1–26. http://doi.org/10.1017/S0047404523000404.

European Commission, Directorate-General for Justice and Consumers, Kaati, L., Cohen, K. & Pelzer, B. (2021). *Heroes and Scapegoats: Right-Wing Extremism*

in Digital Environments. Publications Office of the European Union. https://data
.europa.eu/doi/10.2838/6291.

Europol. (2020). *European Union Terrorism Situation and Trend Report (TE-SAT) 2020*. Luxembourg: European Union. www.europol.europa.eu/cms/
sites/default/files/documents/european_union_terrorism_situation_and_tren
d_report_te-sat_2020_0.pdf.

Europol. (2023). *European Union Terrorism Situation and Trend Report (TE-SAT) 2023*. Luxembourg: European Union. www.europol.europa.eu/cms/
sites/default/files/documents/European%20Union%20Terrorism%20
Situation%20and%20Trend%20report%202023.pdf.

Federal Bureau of Investigation. (2015). Making Prevention a Reality:
Identifying, Assessing, and Managing the Threat of Targeted Attacks. *U.S.
Department of Justice*. www.fbi.gov/file-repository/making-prevention-a-
reality.pdf/view.

Fielitz, M. & Ahmed, R. (2021). It's not funny anymore: Far-right extremists'
use of humour. *Radicalisation Awareness Network*. Luxembourg: European
Union.

Finley, L. & Esposito, L. (2020): Antifa as Bogeyman. *Factis Pax*, 14(2),
105–19.

Fizek, S. & Dippel, A. (2020). Gamification of terror – Power games as liminal
spaces. In M. Groen, N. Kiel , A. Tillmann and A. Weßel, eds., *Games and
Ethics: Theoretical and Empirical Approaches to Ethical Questions in
Digital Game Cultures*. Wiesbaden: Springer VS, pp. 77–94. https://doi
.org/10.1007/978-3-658-28175-5c6.

Freadman, A. (2002). Uptake. In R. Coe, L. Lingard and T. Teslenko, eds., *The
Rhetoric and Ideology of Genre: Strategies for Stability and Change*.
Cresskill: Hampton Press, pp. 39–53.

Freadman, A. (2020). A tardy uptake. *Discourse and Writing/Rédactologie*, 30,
105–32. https://doi.org/10.31468/cjsdwr.781.

Fuchs, C. & Middelhoff, P. (2020). *Das Netzwerk der Neuen Rechten: Wer Sie
Lenkt, Wer Sie Finanziert und Wie Sie die Gesellschaft Verändern*. Reinbek:
Rowohlt Polaris.

Gales, T. (2010). *Ideologies of Violence: A Corpus and Discourse Analytic
Approach to Stance in Threatening Communications*. [Doctoral dissertation,
University of California, Davis]. https://www.proquest.com/openview/
d5725144a44fc7641450382a5672b735/1?pq-origsite=gscholar&cbl=18750.

Gales, T. (2011). Identifying interpersonal stance in threatening discourse: An
appraisal analysis. *Discourse Studies*, 13(1), 27–46. https://doi.org/10.1177/
1461445610387735.

Gales, T. (2015) Threatening stances: A corpus analysis of realized vs. non-realized threats. *Language and Law / Linguagem e Direito*, 2(2), 1–25.

Gales, T. (2019). Threatening contexts: An examination of threatening language from linguistic, legal and law enforcement perspectives. In M. Evans, L. Jeffries and J. O'Driscoll, eds., *The Routledge Handbook of Language in Conflict*. London: Routledge, pp. 472–92. https://doi.org/10.4324/9780429058011-27.

Gales, T. (2021). "Prison has been a proper punishment": Investigating stance in forensic and legal contexts. In M. Coulthard, A. May and R. Sousa-Silva, eds., *The Routledge Handbook of Forensic Linguistics*, 2nd ed. London: Routledge. pp. 675–93.

Genette, G. (1997). *Paratexts: Thresholds of Interpretation*. Cambridge: Cambridge University Press.

Gerster, L., Kuschta, R., Hammer, D. & Schwieter, C. (2021). Stützpfeiler Telegram: Wie Rechtsextreme und Verschwörungsideolog:innen auf Telegram ihre Infrastruktur ausbauen. Berlin: Institute for Strategic Dialogue. www.isdglo bal.org/wp-content/uploads/2021/12/ISD-Germany_Telegram.pdf.

Grice, H. P. (1975). Logic and conversation. In P. Cole and J. L. Morgan, eds., *Speech Acts*. Leiden: Brill, pp. 41–58. https://doi.org/10.1163/97890043 68811_003.

Golem. (2023). *Wikipedia, The Free Encyclopedia*. December 6, https://en .wikipedia.org/w/index.php?title=Golem&oldid=1185971233.

Guhl, J., Ebner, J. & Rau, J. (2020). *The online ecosystem of the German far-right*. London: Institute for Strategic Dialogue. www.isdglobal.org/wp-con tent/uploads/2020/02/ISD-The-Online-Ecosystem-of-the-German-Far-Right-English-Draft-11.pdf.

Guldimann, A. & Meloy, J. R. (2020). Assessing the threat of lone-actor terrorism: The reliability and validity of the TRAP-18. *Forensische Psychiatrie, Psychologie, Kriminologie*, 14(2), pp. 158–66.

Haberl, F. J. (2020). The weapons of choice: Terrorist armament culture and the use of firearms in online propaganda and identity-building through cyber-space. In T. Eze, L. Speakman and C. Onwubiko, eds., *Proceedings of the 19th European Conference on Information Warfare and Security*. Reading, UK: Academic Conferences and Publishing International, pp. 126–35.

Halliday, M. A. K. & Webster, J. (eds.) (2014). *Text Linguistics: The How and Why of Meaning*. Bristol: Equinox.

Halliday, M. A. K. (1978). *Language as Social Semiotic: The Social Interpretation of Language and Meaning*. London: Edward Arnold.

Halliday, M. A. K. & Hasan, R. (2014 [1976]). *Cohesion in English*, 9th ed., New York: Routledge.

Hempel, A., Meloy, J. R. & Richards, T. (1999). Offender and offense characteristics of a nonrandom sample of mass murderers. *Journal of the American Academy of Psychiatry and the Law*, 27(2), 213–25.

Hunter, M. & Grant, T. (2022). Killer stance: An investigation of the relationship between attitudinal resources and psychological traits in the writings of four serial murderers. *Language and Law/Linguagem e Direito*, 9(1), 48–72. https://doi.org/10.21747/21833745/lanlaw/9_1a3.

Hurt, M. (2020). *Pledging To Harm: A Linguistic Analysis of Violent Intent in Threatening Language*. [Doctoral dissertation, Aston University]. https://publi cations.aston.ac.uk/id/eprint/43031/6/HURT_MARLON_DAVID_2020.pdf.

Hurt, M. & Grant, T. (2019). Pledging to harm: A linguistic appraisal analysis of judgment comparing realized and non-realized violent fantasies. *Discourse & Society*, 30(2), 154–71. https://doi.org/10.1177/095792651881619.

Jäger, L., Kracher, V. & Manemann, T. (2021). Fashwave: Rechtsextremer Hass in Retro-Optik. *de:hate report*. Berlin: Amadeu Antonio Stiftung. www.amadeu-antonio-stiftung.de/wpcontent/uploads/2021/06/de.hate_Report02_Fashwave-1.pdf.

Jäger, R. & Landes, M. (2020). Das Leben danach – Das Attentat von Halle. Folge: Der Täter. *Mitteldeutscher Rundfunk*, December 7. www.mdr.de/mdr-sachsen-anhalt/podcast/das-leben-danach/das-attentat-von-halle-100.html.

Keane, W. (2003). Semiotics and the social analysis of material things. *Language & Communication*, 23(3/4), 403–25. https://doi.org/10.1016/S0271-5309(03)00010-7.

Keen, F., Crawford, B. & Suarez-Tangil, G. (2020). *Memetic Irony and the Promotion of Violence within Chan Cultures*. Centre for Research and Evidence on Security Threats. https://crestresearch.ac.uk/resources/memetic-irony-and-the-promotion-of-violence-within-chan-cultures/.

Kiesling, S. F. (2009). Style as stance: Stance as the explanation for patterns of sociolinguistic variation. In A. Jaffe, ed., *Stance: Sociolinguistic Perspectives*. New York: Oxford University Press, pp. 171–94.

Koehler, D. (2019). The Halle, Germany, synagogue attack and the evolution of the far-right terror threat. *CTC Sentinel*, 12(11), 14–20. https://doi.org/10.17606/5z9d-w597.

Kostadinovska-Stojchevska, B. & Shalevska, E. (2018). Internet memes and their socio-linguistic features. *European Journal of Literature, Language and Linguistics Studies*, 2(4), 158–69.

Kriner, M., Barbarossa, E., Bernardo, I. & Broschowitz, M. (2024). *Behind the Skull Mask: An Overview of Militant Accelerationism*. London: Global Network on Extremism and Technology (GNET). https://doi.org/10.18742/pub01-171.

Kriner, M. (2022). An Introduction to Militant Accelerationism. *Accelerationism Research Consortium*, May 9, www.accresearch.org/shortanalysis/an-introduc tion-to-militant-accelerationism.

Kriner, M. & Ihler, B. (2022). Analysing Terrorgram publications: A new digital zine. *Global Network on Extremism and Technology*, September 12. https:// gnet-research.org/2022/09/12/analysing-terrorgram-publications-a-new-digi tal-zine/.

Kruglanski, A., Jasko, K., Webber, D., Chernikova, M. & Molinario, E. (2018). The making of violent extremists. *Review of General Psychology*, 22(1), 107–20.

Kupper, J. (2022). Preventing Attacks Using Targeted Violence Manifestos. *Law Enforcement Bulletin*, May 5. https://leb.fbi.gov/articles/featured-art icles/preventing-attacks-using-targeted-violence-manifestos.

Kupper, J., Christensen, T. K., Wing, D., Hurt, M., Schumacher, M. & Meloy, J. R. (2022). The contagion and copycat effect in transnational far-right terrorism: An analysis of language evidence. *Perspectives on Terrorism*, 16(4), 4–26. www.universiteitleiden.nl/binaries/content/assets/ customsites/perspectives-on-terrorism/2022/issue-4/kupper-et-al.pdf.

Kupper, J., Cotti, P. & Meloy, J. R. (2023). The Hanau terror attack: Unraveling the dynamics of mental disorder and extremist beliefs. *Journal of Threat Assessment and Management*. Advance online publication. https://doi.org/ 10.1037/tam0000201.

Kupper, J. & Dittrich, M. (2023). The Reichsbürger coup: How the German covid-19 denier scene and anti-lockdown movement became a breeding ground for terrorism. *Global Network on Extremism and Technology*, January 18. https://gnet-research.org/2023/01/18/the-reichsburger-coup-how-the-german-covid-19-denier-scene-and-anti-lockdown-movement-became-a-breeding-ground-for-terrorism/.

Kupper, J. & Dittrich, M. (2024). Terrorgram's propaganda: An overview of publications designed to incite accelerationist terrorism attacks. *Accelerationism Research Consortium*. https://www.accresearch.org/accre ports/terrorgrams-propaganda-an-overview-of-publications-designed-to-incite-accelerationist-terrorism-attacks.

Kupper, J. & Meloy, J. R. (2021). TRAP-18 indicators validated through the forensic linguistic analysis of targeted violence manifestos. *Journal of Threat Assessment and Management*, 8(4), 174–99.

Kupper, J. & Meloy, J. R. (2023). *Going Dark: The Inverse Relationship between Online and On-the-Ground Pre-offence Behaviours in Targeted Attackers*. London: Global Network on Extremism and Technology. https:// doi.org/10.18742/pub01-162.

Kupper, J., Rękawek K. & Kriner, M. (2023). Terrorgram's first saint: Analyzing accelerationist terrorism in Bratislava. *Accelerationism Research Consortium*, March 29. https://static1.squarespace.com/static/6193e52959704a0c3b5b4b0c/t/6421ecf5721fc579c2799737/1679944949837/ARC_Terrorgrams+First+Saint_Bratislava.pdf.

Langman, P. (2009). *Why Kids Kill: Inside the Minds of School Shooters*. New York: Palgrave Macmillan.

Leary, M. R., Kowalski, R. M., Smith, L. & Phillips, S. (2003). Teasing, rejection, and violence: Case studies of the school shootings. *Aggressive Behavior*, 29(3), 202–14. https://doi.org/10.1002/ab.10061.

Levinson, S. C. (1983). *Pragmatics*. Cambridge: Cambridge University Press.

Luckham, R. (1984). Armament culture. *Alternatives*, 10, 1–44.

Lunds Tingsrätt. (2021). Förundersökningsprotokoll, B4482-21 Aktbilaga 64, October 2021. [Lund district court, preliminary investigation report].

Macklin, G. (2022). Praise the saints. In J. Dafinger and M. Florin, eds., *A Transnational History of Right-Wing Terrorism: Political Violence and the Far Right in Eastern and Western Europe since 1900*. Abingdon: Routledge, pp. 216–40. https://doi.org/10.4324/9781003105251-16.

Manemann, T. (2020). *Rechtsterroristische Online-Subkulturen: Analysen und Handlungsempfehlungen*. Berlin: Amadeu Antonio Stiftung. www.amadeu-antonio-stiftung.de/wp-content/uploads/2021/02/Broschu%CC%88re-Rechtsterroristische-Online-Subkulturen_pdf.pdf.

Martens, W. H. J. (2014). The hidden suffering of the psychopath. *Psychiatric Times*, 13(10). www.psychiatrictimes.com/view/hidden-suffering-psychopath.

Martin, J. R. & White, P. R. R. (2005) *The Language of Evaluation: Appraisal in English*. New York: Palgrave/Macmillan.

Martin, J. R. (2004). Sense and sensibility: Texturing evaluation. In J. Foley, ed., *Language, Education and Discourse*. London: Continuum, pp. 270–304.

Meguca. (2019). Thread *Meadhall*.

Meloy, J. R. Sheridan, K. & Hoffman, J. (2008). Public figure stalking, threats, and attacks: The state of the science. In J. R. Meloy, L. Sheridan and J. Hoffmann, eds., *Stalking, Threatening, and Attacking Public Figures: A Psychological and Behavioral Analysis*. New York: Oxford University Press, pp. 435–55.

Meloy, J. R., Hoffmann, J., Guldimann, A. & James, D. (2012). The role of warning behaviors in threat assessment: An exploration and suggested typology. *Behavioral Sciences and the Law*, 30(3), 256–79.

Meloy, J. R., Hoffmann, J., Roshdi, K., Glaz-Ocik, J. & Guldimann, A. (2014). Warning behaviors and their configurations across various domains of targeted violence. In R. Meloy and J. Hoffman, eds., *International Handbook of Threat Assessment*. New York: Oxford University Press, pp. 39–53.

Meloy, J. R., Hempel, A., Mohandie, K., Gray, T., Shiva, A. & Richards, T. (2004). A comparative analysis of North American adolescent and adult mass murderers. *Behavioral Sciences and the Law*, 22, 291–309.

Miller, C. R. (1984). Genre as social action. *Quarterly Journal of Speech*, 70(2), 151–67. https://doi.org/10.1080/00335638409383686.

Miller, C. R. (2015). Genre change and evolution. In N. Artemeva and A. Freedman, eds., *Genre Studies around the Globe, beyond the Three Traditions*. Bloomington: Trafford Publications, pp. 154–85.

Mitteldeutscher Rundfunk. (2019). Anschlag in Halle: Stahlknecht schildert genauen Ablauf. *Mitteldeutscher Rundfunk*. www.mdr.de/nachrichten/sach sen-anhalt/halle/halle/pressekonferenz-stahlknecht-zu-anschlag-halle-100 .html.

Mohandie, K. & Meloy, J. R. (2013). The value of crime scene and site visitation by forensic psychologists and psychiatrists. *Journal of Forensic Sciences*, 58(3), 719–23. https://doi.org/10.1111/1556-4029.12135.

Musu, L., Zhang, A., Wang, K., Jizhi, Z. & Oudekerk, B. A. (2019). *Indicators of School Crime and Safety: 2018*. Institute of Education Sciences National Center for Education Statistics. U.S. Department of Education, and Bureau of Justice Statistics, Office of Justice Programs, U.S. Department of Justice. Washington, DC. https://nces.ed.gov/pubs2019/2019047.pdf.

Norrick, N. (2010). Humor in interaction. *Language and Linguistics Compass*, 4(4), 232–44. https://doi.org/10.1111/j.1749-818X.2010.00189.x.

Norris, J. J. (2024). Could the futility of terrorism inspire deradicalization? Narrative strategies arising from case studies of far-right lone-actor terrorism. *Journal for Deradicalization*, (38), 28–80.

Nyboe, J. (2016). The game of the name: Genre labels as genre and signature. *Scandinavian Studies*, 88(4), 364–392. https://doi.org/ 10.5406/scanstud.88.4.0364.

O'Toole, M. E. & Smith, S. S. (2014). Fundamentals of threat assessment for beginners. *International Handbook of Threat Assessment*. New York: Oxford University Press.

O'Toole, M. E., Smith, S. S. & Hare, R. D. (2008). Psychopathy and predatory stalking of public figures. In J. R. Meloy, L. Sheridan and J. Hoffmann, eds., *Stalking, Threatening, and Attacking Public Figures*. New York: Oxford University Press, pp. 215–43.

Ochs, E. (1992). Indexing gender. In A. Duranti and C. Goodwin, eds., *Rethinking Context*. Cambridge [England]; New York: Cambridge University Press, pp. 335–58.

Papadopulos, M. (2022). Von digitalem Hass zu analoger Gewalt. Bedrohun gsmanagement 'onlife' – Destruktive Dynamiken in und aus Online-Räumen. *Kriminalistik*, 05/22, pp. 277–83.

Perliger, A. (2020). *American Zealots: Inside Right-Wing Domestic Terrorism.* New York: Columbia University Press.

Pook, L., Stanjek, G. & Wigard, T. (2021). *Der Halle-Prozess: Mitschriften.* Leipzig: Spector Books. https://spectorbooks.com/book/der-halle-prozess-mitschriften.

Ray, A., Plante, C. N., Reysen, S., Roberts, S. E. & Gerbasi, K. C. (2017). Psychological needs predict fanship and fandom in anime fans. *The Phoenix Papers*, 3(1), 56–68.

Schattka, C. (2020). Halle (Saale), 9. Oktober 2019. Protokoll eines Anschlags. *Zeitschrift des Hamburger Instituts für Sozialforschung, Mittelweg 36*, 29(4/5), 45–62.

Schwarz, K. (2020). *Hasskrieger: Der neue globale Rechtsextremismus.* Freiburg: Verlag Herder.

Scrivens, R., Wojciechowski, T. W., Freilich, J. D., Chermak, S. M. & Frank, R. (2021). Comparing the online posting behaviors of violent and non-violent right-wing extremists. *Terrorism and Political Violence*, 35(1), 192–209. https://doi.org/10.1080/09546553.2021.1891893.

Searle, J. R. (1979). A taxonomy of illocutionary acts. In *Expression and Meaning: Studies in The Theory of Speech Acts*, vol. I. Cambridge: Cambridge University Press, pp. 1–29.

Searle, J. R. (2008 [1965]). What is a speech act. In I. Hutchby, ed., *Methods in Language and Social Interaction*. Thousand Oaks: Sage, pp. 1–16.

Sebba, M. (2012). Orthography as social action: Scripts, spelling, identity and power. In A. Jaffe, J. Androutsopoulos, M. Sebba and S. Johnson, eds., *Orthography as Social Action: Scripts, Spelling, Identity and Power.* Berlin: Walter de Gruyter, pp. 1–20.

Senate Rules Committee. (2016). *California Legislative Information, SB 1189 Senate Bill.* www.leginfo.ca.gov/pub/15-16/bill/sen/sb_1151-1200/sb_1189_cfa_20160531_094703_sen_floor.html.

Shuy, R. W. (2003). Discourse analysis in the legal context. In D. Tannen, H. E. Hamilton and D. Schiffrin, eds., *The Handbook of Discourse Analysis*, 2nd ed. Oxford: Wiley Blackwell, pp. 822–40.

Shuy, R. W. (2015). Discourse analysis in the legal context. In D. Tannen, H. E. Hamilton and D. Schiffrin, eds., *The Handbook of Discourse Analysis*, 2nd ed. Malden: John Wiley & Sons, 822–40.

Simi, P. & Windisch, S. (2020). The culture of violent talk: An interpretive approach. *Social Sciences*, 9(7), 1–16. https://doi.org/10.3390/socsci9070120.

Simons, A. & Tunkel, R. F. (2021). The assessment of anonymous threatening communications. In J. R. Meloy and J. H. Hoffman, eds., *International Handbook of Threat Assessment*, 2nd ed. New York: Oxford University Press, pp. 235–56.

Smith, S. S., O'Toole, M. E. & Hare, R. D. (2012). The predator: When the stalker is a psychopath. *FBI Law Enforcement Bulletin*, 81(7), 9–13.

Smith, S. S., Woyach, R. B. & O'Toole, M.E. (2014). Threat triage: How to recognize the needle in the stack of disturbing and threatening communications. In J. R. Meloy and J. Hoffmann, eds., *International Handbook of Threat Assessment*. New York: Oxford University Press, pp. 321–9.

Smith, S. S. & Young, M. D. (2021). Threat triage: Recognizing the needle in the haystack. In J. R. Meloy and J. Hoffmann, eds., *International Handbook of Threat Assessment*. New York: Oxford University Press, pp. 507–21.

Squire, K. D. (2014). Video-game literacy: A literacy of expertise. In J. Coiro, M. Knobel, C. Lankshear and D. J. Leu, eds., *Handbook of Research on New Literacies*. New York: Routledge, pp. 635–70.

Striegel, S. (2021). *Bericht des 19: Parlamentarischen Untersuchungsausschusses*. Landtag von Sachsen-Anhalt, Magdeburg. https://padoka.landtag.sachsen-anhalt.de/files/drs/wp7/drs/d7575vbt.pdf.

Swales, J. (1990). *Genre Analysis: English in Academic and Research Settings*. Cambridge: Cambridge University Press.

Swales, J. M. (2016). Reflections on the concept of discourse community. *Asp la revue du GERAS*, 69, 7–19. https://doi.org/10.4000/asp.4774.

Tajfel, H. & Turner, J. C. (1979) An integrative theory of intergroup conflict. *The Social Psychology of Intergroup Relations*, 33(47), 33–27. Monterey, CA: Brooks and Cole.

Thompson, C. (2015). *The Soul of Shame*. Downers Grove: InterVarsity Press.

Thorleifsson, C. & Düker, J. (2021). Lone actors in digital environments. *Radicalisation Awareness Network*. Luxembourg: European Union. https://home-affairs.ec.europa.eu/system/files/2021-10/ran_paper_lone_actors_in_digital_environments_en.pdf.

Vagle, W. & Wikberg, K. (2001). *New Directions in Nordic Text Linguistics and Discourse Analysis: Methodological Issues*. Oslo: Novus.

Van der Meer, B., Meloy, J. R. & Hoffmann, J. (2017). The adult mass murderer in Europe and North America: The paranoid spectrum from distrust to delusion. Presentation at *the 27th Annual Threat Management Conference of Association of Threat Assessment Professionals*. Anaheim, California. https://secureservercdn.net/72.167.243.77/66f.213.myftpupload.com/wp-content/uploads/2017/08/ATAP2017.pdf.

Van Dijk, T. A. (1977). *Text and Context. Explorations in the Semantics and Pragmatics of Discourse*. London: Longman.

von Berg, A. (2019). Risk Assessment im Phänomenbereich gewaltbereiter Extremismus – State of the Art. *Interventionen*, 13, 4–15.

Wahlström, M. (2020). Chatten, hetzen, töten. Radikalisierung als Lernprozess. *Mittelweg 36. Zeitschrift des Hamburger Instituts für* Sozialforschung, 29, 63–80.

Webb, J. (2022). Warriors and Waifus: Community responses to historical accuracy and the representation of women in total war: Three kingdoms. In J. Draycott, ed., *Women in Historical and Archaeological Video Games*. Berlin: De Gruyter, pp. 101–38.

Weber, S. (2018). White supremacy's old gods: The far right and neopaganism. *Political Research Associates*. February 1. https://politicalresearch.org/2018/02/01/white-supremacys-old-gods-the-far-right-and-neopaganism.

Welt. (2022). Halle-Attentäter nach Geiselnahme in bayrisches Gefängnis verlegt. *Welt.de*, www.welt.de/politik/deutschland/article242790225/Halle-Attentaeter-nach-Geiselnahme-in-Bayern-inhaftiert.html.

Wenger, E., McDermott, R. & Snyder, W. (2002). *Cultivating Communities of Practice: A Guide to Managing Knowledge*. Boston: Harvard Business School Press.

White, P. R. R. (2015). *The Appraisal Website: The Language of Attitude, Arguability, and Interpersonal Positioning*, April 8, 2024. www.grammatics.com/appraisal/

White, S. G. & Meloy, J. R. (2016). *The WAVR-21: Workplace Assessment of Violence Risk Including Campus and Student Contexts*, 3rd ed., San Diego: Specialized Training.

Wing, D. (2017). *The Progression of Interpersonal Stances in the Writings of School Shooters*. [Master thesis, Hofstra University]. ProQuest. https://www.proquest.com/openview/bcc29d777c8ebe9e9beb04a9eb86c942/1?pq-origsite=gscholar&cbl=18750.

Wray, C. (2021). *Threats to the Homeland: Evaluating the Landscape 20 Years after 9/11*. Statement before the Senate Homeland Security and Governmental Affairs Committee, September 21. Washington, DC: Federal Bureau of Investigation. www.fbi.gov/news/testimony/threats-to-the-homeland-evaluating-the-landscape-20-years-after-911-wray-092121.

Acknowledgments

We thank Dr. Marlon Hurt for his early contributions to this Element, particularly his assistance with the interrater reliability of the appraisal analysis. We also thank the editors, Tammy Gales and Tim Grant, and the reviewers for their invaluable feedback.

Cambridge Elements ☰

Forensic Linguistics

Tim Grant

Aston University

Tim Grant is Professor of Forensic Linguistics, Director of the Aston Institute for Forensic Linguistics, and past president of the International Association of Forensic Linguists. His recent publications have focussed on online sexual abuse conversations including *Language and Online Identities: The Undercover Policing of Internet Sexual Crime* (with Nicci MacLeod, Cambridge, 2020).

Tim is one of the world's most experienced forensic linguistic practitioners and his case work has involved the analysis of abusive and threatening communications in many different contexts including investigations into sexual assault, stalking, murder, and terrorism. He also makes regular media contributions including presenting police appeals such as for the BBC Crimewatch programme.

Tammy Gales

Hofstra University

Tammy Gales is Professor of Linguistics and the Director of Research at the Institute for Forensic Linguistics, Threat Assessment, and Strategic Analysis at Hofstra University, New York. She has served on the Executive Committee for the International Association of Forensic Linguists (IAFL), is on the editorial board for the peer-reviewed journals Applied Corpus Linguistics and Language and Law / Linguagem e Direito, and is a member of the advisory board for the BYU Law and Corpus Linguistics group. Her research interests cross the boundaries of forensic linguistics and language and the law, with a primary focus on threatening communications. She has trained law enforcement agents from agencies across Canada and the U.S. and has applied her work to both criminal and civil cases.

About the Series

Elements in Forensic Linguistics provides high-quality accessible writing, bringing cutting-edge forensic linguistics to students and researchers as well as to practitioners in law enforcement and law. Elements in the series range from descriptive linguistics work, documenting a full range of legal and forensic texts and contexts; empirical findings and methodological developments to enhance research, investigative advice, and evidence for courts; and explorations into the theoretical and ethical foundations of research and practice in forensic linguistics

Cambridge Elements ≡

Forensic Linguistics

Elements in the Series

The Idea of Progress in Forensic Authorship Analysis
Tim Grant

Forensic Linguistics in the Philippines: Origins, Developments, and Directions
Marilu Rañosa-Madrunio, Isabel Pefianco Martin

The Language of Fake News
Jack Grieve, Helena Woodfield

A Theory of Linguistic Individuality for Authorship Analysis
Andrea Nini

Forensic Linguistics in Australia: Origins, Progress and Prospects
Diana Eades, Helen Fraser, Georgina Heydon

Online Child Sexual Grooming Discourse
Nuria Lorenzo-Dus, Craig Evans and Ruth Mullineux-Morgan

Spoken Threats from Production to Perception
James Tompkinson

Authorship Analysis in Chinese Social Media Texts
Shaomin Zhang

The Language of Romance Crimes: Interactions of Love, Money, and Threat
Elisabeth Carter

Legal-Lay Discourse and Procedural Justice in Family and County Courts
Tatiana Grieshofer

Forensic Linguistics in China: Origins, Progress, and Prospects
Yuan Chuanyou, Xu Youping and Lu Nan

Decoding Terrorism: An Interdisciplinary Approach to a Lone-Actor Case
Julia Kupper, Marie Bojsen-Møller, Tanya Karoli Christensen, Dakota Wing,
Marcus Papadopulos and Sharon Smith

A full series listing is available at: www.cambridge.org/EIFL

Printed in the United States
by Baker & Taylor Publisher Services